To Eithne

Ed iLaughlin

THE LAST GOOD FUNERAL
OF THE YEAR

THE LAST GOOD FUNERAL OF THE YEAR

Ed O'Loughlin

riverrun

First published in Great Britain in 2022 by

riverrun
An imprint of

Quercus Editions Ltd
Carmelite House
50 Victoria Embankment
London EC4Y 0DZ

An Hachette UK company

A CIP catalogue record for this book is available
from the British Library

Hardback ISBN 978 1 52941 706 7
Ebook ISBN 978 1 52941 708 1

10 9 8 7 6 5 4 3 2

Typeset by CC Book Production
Printed and bound in Great Britain by Clays Ltd, Elcograf S.p.A.

Papers used by riverrun are from well-managed forests and other responsible sources.

For my father

Hindsight is twenty-twenty

Modern English proverb

February

Undecided

You're not doing that right, she told him, as she watched him from the bed.

He stopped and turned to look at her. Or maybe he hadn't turned to look at her. Maybe he found her reflection in the mirror, foregrounded by the razor he held in his hand. That's how a writer would frame it.

What are you talking about?

You're not meant to shave like that. You're meant to do it smoothly.

He stared at her, incredulous. He knew she could be bossy, but this was too much.

What do *you* know about shaving your face?

She had shaved her legs and armpits, of course. And she

must have seen it on TV, in the commercials. A handsome man draws a razor in a long, smooth pass through a perfect mask of shaving foam, exposing a line of tan skin. No scraping motions, no nervous sawing away at the same patch of face – which was how he shaved: back and forth, up and down, the way most people brush their teeth.

Try it, she said.

She would have bounced in the bed as she said it; her enthusiasm always took physical form. She would have raised her voice as they bickered, still delighted with each other. She would have laughed at him. She had a brash, happy laugh.

Seriously. Try doing it more smoothly.

And in the end he did. And it worked. But it was too late for her. Her chin was already raw from the beard rash.

He remembered the bed in their guest house as narrow, but all beds feel narrow at that age, when you seldom roll far apart. So he could be wrong now, twenty-seven years later, about the width of that bed. But he did remember the nights they had spent there, and how they had felt. He remembered her telling him how to shave better. And he remembered their room in that Donegal guest house, two faces in a mirror, a pattern of light, the placement of the bed with a window to the right of it. But he couldn't remember what town it was in. He had an idea it was Moville. Though it might have been Carndonagh.

They drove up from Dublin in his first car, the one he'd bought at a police auction, and later that day they crossed Inishowen to Lough Swilly. By the shore in Buncrana, in the cold rain from the west, an old fisherman delighted her with stories of his life at sea – she loved talking to strangers, which was something he dreaded – but twenty-seven years later, those stories were gone.

In Derry, on the way home, she saw candy-striped shirts outside a pub near the Bogside. Derry City were playing Shelbourne, from Dublin, in a League of Ireland soccer match. She decided she wanted to go. When she wanted to do something, she usually did it. She was always curious, always looking for something new. He was reluctant, but they went to the game in the Brandywell anyway, and it was fun. It usually was, with her.

And twenty-seven years later, when it became suddenly urgent for him to gather all the fragments that he had of Charlotte McDonald, to establish the timelines, he remembered this match, and realised that it was a beacon, a quasar, a point he could fix in lost space and time. To determine exactly when they had gone north for that weekend, he could look up the football records online.

Derry City played Shelbourne at home in the Brandywell on Sunday, 1 November 1992, a little over a month short of his twenty-sixth birthday.

No kick-off time was given, but he could remember the floodlights and the chill in the air. Had he really agreed to drive the four hours back to Dublin in the dark, late at night, during the Troubles, on the old bad roads, through the border at Aughnacloy, just so she could watch a semi-professional football match? She wasn't even that big a fan of football. You had to hand it to Charlotte: what she wanted, she usually got.

The records said that the match finished scoreless, though he could have sworn he remembered a goal. What did he really remember about his time with Charlotte McDonald?

The first of November 1992. That at least was a start. He put that into the timeline. He had come to remember their thing, more or less fondly, as a summer fling, but now that he checked it was winter and fall.

Charlotte had graduated two years before with a degree in law that she no longer wanted. She had gone to live in France with a boyfriend, and she had come back to Dublin without him. Having just turned twenty-four, she moved back in with her parents and younger siblings. She was weightless then, undecided, no job and no plans. She could have become anything, and that's how he would always remember her. As it turned out, she would start her own business, in a creative industry, and she would do very well.

His phone pinged, on the table, to the left of his laptop, twenty-seven years later. Without picking up the phone, he glanced at its screen and then closed his eyes. Charlotte, he said. He had a sense of something coming gently loose inside him, of a subroutine that had been running for decades, unnoticed in the background, revealing its existence by the act of shutting down.

Later that night, he called Charlotte's cell phone. He assumed it would have been switched off by then, that his call would go to voicemail, and that he'd hear her bored voice, one last time, telling him to leave a message and that she would get back to him. But instead it started ringing, so he ended the call before somebody answered. He'd used this trick before, twenty years ago, calling his brother's Nokia. But back then he'd known for sure that no one would answer: his brother, unlike Charlotte, had lived and died alone.

It occurred to him now, at ten thirty-five p.m. on the night of Charlotte's death, that someone, at some point, and most likely her husband, would pick up Charlotte's phone and see the message on the screen: *Missed call*, and the time it was made, and most likely his name: he and Charlotte had each other's numbers, though they never used them anymore. He hoped that her husband, whom he liked, would understand. And when her husband later replied to his email of condolence, a couple of days later, he made no mention of any posthumous phone calls. *Thanks for getting in touch*, he said.

The fact was projected on to his ceiling that first night, and for many nights thereafter: he should have known that Charlotte was dying. It turned out she had been very sick for several months. He should have been in contact with her. He should have said – what? Goodbye? No. He should have said hello. Even just an email or a text. *Get well. Thinking of you.* That would have been enough. It was too late now. Now he was trapped in the dark at night, trying to save what he could of her. And he despised himself for this, because he knew he had no right to have strong feelings about her, just because she was suddenly dead. He had checked that already: it had been twenty-seven years. They hadn't even been in love back then. He had acquired his own people since, a real life, and a good one, and had suffered real losses of his own. He told himself this from the start: this wasn't just about Charlotte. It was about him suddenly being faced with facts he'd been ignoring – that he was getting old, that he wasn't what he used to be, that his imagination, always overactive, had at some point reversed its direction, switching production from dreams to regrets. Anyone could see the gears turning, the facile clockwork. It was selfish and dishonest. And worse, it was dull.

Charlotte herself had been no sentimentalist. If she could see him like this, she'd be shaking her head in sorrow while trying hard not to laugh. And she would have blurted out what he understood to be true but would not want to hear said aloud: that it was himself he was mourning the most, not her. Plus, he knew perfectly well that this was one-sided, that she would not have thought about him, one of several old boyfriends, from one year to the next. He didn't think she was one for regrets.

And yet the pain *felt* real enough. As real as those other times, when he *had* been entitled. Is phantom pain ever really a thing? Surely if it hurts, it hurts? And maybe there was something real underneath all the nonsense, some real basis for grieving. So he found himself searching his emails, texts, the Internet, his memory, for evidence in his defence.

When, for a start, had he last actually seen her? It seemed like a couple of years ago. He checked that now. It had been over six years. They'd had coffee together at her workshop in Ringsend. This was his last confirmed meeting with Charlotte. Six years. It was possible they'd run into each other somewhere after that, as you do in Dublin, but if so, he'd forgotten. Which didn't help his case.

They had agreed, that last time, that she would bring her kids over to his house some afternoon, to meet his kids, and they would all go together to the Botanic Gardens. He realised that he still had that vague date with her in the back of his head. It was where he had parked her, and she had parked him. Then he remembered that he had also invited her to an event of his, three years ago. Had she come? He checked his emails. She had accepted the invitation, then not turned up, and had sent apologies later that night. Things were hectic, she said. Moving house.

The last time they'd exchanged messages of any sort was two years before her death. He'd heard that she'd made a big score in her business, and emailed her his congratulations. She had answered straight away.

Lovely to hear from you! I'm delighted with the new gig!! . . . See you soon I hope C

By then, he knew now, she'd been living for a year with cancer in her lungs.

Two days after Charlotte's death, he passed his wife in the kitchen. And she said to him, quietly, Are you all right?

He stopped, his back still to her.

No. I don't think I am.

He turned to face her.

I'm upset about Charlotte. I know that it's just some midlife bullshit, that it's because she's the first of my old girlfriends to die. We were never in love, not even then. It didn't last long, and there was no unfinished business between us. But I do feel very sad about her. I'm sorry. I'll get over it soon.

Every word of this was true, as he said it. But this was his wife, the mother of their two children. She stared back at him, mistrustful. She would have to believe him, though he'd let her down before.

OK, she said slowly. But I think you're being self-indulgent.

He thought, You won't get any arguments from me.

While he could tell himself, from the start, that this wasn't all, or even mostly, about Charlotte, he fretted that there might still be something of her, something that he'd shut off or forgotten, still tangled up in his life. He couldn't just turn away without an investigation. He had to become a detective, to figure out what good reasons he had, if any, for missing her now, when they were nothing to each other, and he hadn't seen her for years.

Start with the young things . . . He didn't get his first mobile phone until a year after his time with her ended. The Internet and email came a year later still. Cameras had film in them, then, and neither of them carried one. So far as he knew, there were no photographs, no visual record at all, of their time together. They had been, in a way, among the last of their kind. To see them together again, as they were then, he had only his memory.

He remembered her as quite tall, and physically restless. She told him she had been a swimmer as a girl, for her school, or some club in the city. He still saw that in her figure. She had sea-coloured eyes, a wide mouth with strong lips, high cheeks, good skin. Her default expression was a slightly sardonic, slightly skew smile. Her hair was a deep matt brown, straight and thick, worn shortish or mid-length. He remembered how soft it was at the nape. She used to worry then that it was oily. It was a little oily, but he had liked the way it felt.

She liked to wear Lycra dresses when they went out for the evening. She told him that Lycra, which was then at the height of fashion, was her favourite fabric. She liked the way it snapped back into shape after she stretched it. She wore Lycra well.

When Charlotte stayed over with him, they often went swimming next morning in a nearby pool. That was her idea. The pool was operated by a medical charity, and was intended mainly for people with poor health or limited mobility, so the water was always too warm. They splashed about in it, getting some exercise, and sometimes they would furtively embrace, if the lifeguard wasn't watching, and then separate quickly, before things went too far. He remembered the feel of her, slippy and strong in the lukewarm water. Her one-piece suit was made of Lycra too. In the water she felt weightless.

He remembered how she had fretted that one of her legs

was bigger than the other. Or perhaps it was one of her breasts – he couldn't remember, twenty-seven years later. Either way, he hadn't been able to see any difference, and had told her that at the time. When he'd last talked with her face to face, at her workshop, she told him that she'd just had a scare with breast cancer, but she was in the clear, now, and the prognosis was good. The doctors said she would probably live out her span. Fingers crossed.

For years, when he thought of her at all, he liked to tell himself that he and Charlotte had not been suited anyway. She was kind and warm and fun-loving. Enthusiastic. Fearless. Forthright. Impulsive. Everyone said so. He was introverted, inflexible, inhibited, inclined to laziness and envy, slow to get started, though dogged enough when he did. They would never have lasted, and she had duly dumped him.

But now that he thought back, it hadn't been quite that one-sided. Now, when he thought about it, late at night, he could remember having had his own reservations about Charlotte. She was very nice, but somewhat bossy. He remembered telling himself that, towards the end (though he hadn't seen that end coming). She was very attractive, and positive, and fun to be with. She was a great person. She would do. He had actually told himself that. Charlotte would do. But there had been something missing in their relationship for him as well. She didn't seem to have a dark place, or none that he could find. And he was of an age, and temperament, and generation, to confuse darkness with depth. Sometimes, untroubled by doubt – on the surface at least – Charlotte had seemed to him a little unimaginative. Later, watching her career develop, he had conceived her as someone who could be happy as a big fish in a small pond. He was the other way around. For most of his life, he had fetishised horizons. They were never meant to be.

He set out in good time for the funeral in Malahide, taking the car on to the M50. But there was a sign flashing at the entrance ramp to the motorway, too late for him to turn away. *Traffic accident ahead, long delays expected.* Tail lights appeared almost immediately, backed up all the way south from the airport interchange. He arrived at the funeral half an hour late, hating himself to the point of being ill.

Her husband was already speaking when he got there, but the church was full and he couldn't go inside. He had to stay in the churchyard, listening to the service on the speakers. It was a bright, breezy morning, and people stood and listened as her husband delivered an unscripted eulogy, moving and funny, about the foibles and virtues of a beloved wife and mother, their family's force of nature. People were laughing inside the church. He was smiling too.

Yet from one of her husband's passing remarks, he learned that Charlotte had been in a wheelchair towards the end. It stopped his breath for a moment. He couldn't imagine her in a wheelchair. And he thought, Well, that ache at least is true and good. There *was* something selfless mixed in with his bullshit.

He couldn't imagine Charlotte McDonald surrendering to other forces of nature. He knew how that felt, and he didn't think it was for her. When he was sixteen years old, a chronic asthmatic and secret smoker, he'd been hospitalised with severe bronchitis, put on oxygen, and, when the drugs no longer worked, nurses had offered useless suggestions, folk remedies, better ways to draw breath. After hours of this, he got tired. Breathing was agony, burning pains in his ribs and his back. His muscles were failing. So he found himself doing something that he had read about in books, and had assumed was just a myth, or a figure of speech. He had turned his face to the wall. He was waiting to die, and he wasn't even frightened. He was just very tired and sore.

He wondered, listening to the voice on the speaker, how it had been for Charlotte in the end. And something came to him then that was also a comfort, something else that was good and true: if *he* hadn't been frightened, then neither had she.

Afterwards, everyone agreed that the eulogy had been as uplifting a talk as you could possibly hear at the funeral of a mother taken so young. But he didn't feel uplifted. Standing outside, in the sunshine and breeze, he was battered by a new wave of confusion. Where did this come from? This funeral was meant to have done its job. All the words had been said.

But her husband's speech had made him realise that he couldn't simply forget Charlotte now, as he'd hoped, consign her to the life she had led, the years that had changed her, the half-stranger that he had assumed she'd become. Because, from what her husband had said, she hadn't changed at all. She was still the same person he'd known, all those years ago. He'd heard her laugh, too, when her husband was talking. The old Charlotte had lived, however remotely, with however many new layers of accretion, until five days before.

The service was over. He saw all Charlotte's people spill out of the church, and he shamefully forgot about his own family, the real one, and he felt alone. Soon, the lockdown would start. People would die alone in isolation wards, with no one there to hold their hands, and be buried alone, without any proper ceremony. Charlotte's death would be washed away, the first drop in a downpour. But for now, emerging into the windy sunshine, all was as it had ever been. Irish people go to funerals. They circle the wagons, count the survivors. Everyone could still hug and kiss, wipe away the tears and snot, shake hands with her husband, her family, her kids. Nobody knew it then, but this would be the last good funeral of the year.

He remembered how he used to drive out to get Charlotte from her family home. Years later, he would still instinctively glance at the turn that he no longer took, on the rare occasions when he drove out that way. Right from the start, she would bring him into the house to meet her charming family. He had liked this very much; it made him feel special. Now, he realised that she must have taken all her boyfriends back to meet her parents, right from the start. She was always so up front. Everyone said that she held nothing back. That was certainly true. She spoke her mind, and she had a gift for punching through his reserve which he found that he liked, especially in their rare later meetings. The last time they'd met, drinking coffee together in her workshop, she had brought up another of his old relationships, a mutual friend. Charlotte announced to him, typically matter of fact, that she knew he'd hurt her friend, but also that the break-up had been hard on him too.

She said that life could be messy, but they all had their own lives now, and children. It had all ended well. So now that he thought back, he had another good reason for missing Charlotte McDonald. She alone from that time had offered some forgiveness. He didn't realise it until it was too late, but she had been his last link, though half-forgotten, in the background, to some other not-quite-finished business. He had just lost his only friendly witness.

There was an announcement on the speakers outside the church. The burial would be for family only, but afterwards all were welcome for drinks at a nearby hotel.

He walked down to the shops, bought a packet of cigarettes, though he hadn't smoked for years, smoked two on the pavement, got in his car and drove home. Do your own time, A. C. Newman advised from the car stereo. Go back to your own kind.

This time, the M50 was clear. At home, he said hello to his children, who were now back from school, left the car for his wife, who would drive them to Girl Guides, which was usually his job, and took a bus into town. At Tara Street, he got on the DART train back to Malahide. It took him past Killester, where he and Charlotte used to board the train when they went into town together. It was getting dark now, and the rain and strong wind had returned: act two of Storm Ciara. A force of nature. Why not Storm Charlotte? he thought.

The hotel faced the sea. Wind and rain lashed the front, where some people were smoking. He joined them, smoked, then went inside. Already, the smoke was clawing his lungs. It made him feel young again.

The hotel was crowded, a lot of faces from the old days. It turned out, everyone had known for months that Charlotte was very sick and probably wouldn't make it. Even some of those to whom he was still close, whom he still met for drinks in town now and then. No one had thought to mention it to him. This was Dublin. They'd just assumed that he would know too. Plus, it wasn't as if he and Charlotte were close.

Young children ran wild in this forest of adults, playing their games. He looked at them closely, wondering which two were Charlotte's, which were her nephews and nieces. He never found out. Later, when he was talking to her husband, he found him to be pretty cheerful, considering. But of course, he was drinking too, and he'd been through a lot, for months and for years, and this was his respite. He was now in the eye of Storm Charlotte.

What he heard himself say, a little too drunk, maybe:

You know, we still saw each other sometimes, for a while

after we broke up. But it was never serious. We were never in love. There was never any unfinished business between us.

The timeline was settled, the charges drawn up. The formal phase of their relationship lasted only four months – September, October, November, December.

It had its beginning, and end, in Prague. One August, he had gone there to visit a friend, Robert, who had a flat near the middle of the city. Robert had been friends with Charlotte at college, and he rhapsodised about how fun she was, and kind, and also how beautiful. If Robert hadn't been gay, Robert said, he would have been in love with Charlotte himself.

They'd all gone to the same college, but he hadn't known either Robert or Charlotte at that time. He had seen her around the arts block, though, and he had recognised her at once when a friend first introduced them, not long after Charlotte had graduated. Charlotte was someone you noticed around.

Shortly after he got back to Dublin from Prague, he phoned her, to relay some message from Robert. Or maybe that was the pretext. They agreed they should meet up sometime for a drink. He couldn't remember whose initiative that was, but he thought it was probably hers. She was the direct one.

They went for a drink in the pub, and then a late dinner in Blazes, a restaurant that served alcohol late, which very few places in Dublin did then. They drank and talked enough to make things easy, and when the place closed, in the small hours of the morning, they kissed on the pavement outside. He remembered looking at her, in wonder, and asking her why this was happening. And she laughed at the question and said, Oh, you know, you see someone around who you think is good looking, and you say to yourself, Maybe I'll end up with them.

They had in fact had one proper fight, before the official break-up. He only remembered it now, when she was dead. It was just before they went to Prague together to celebrate New Year's Eve, to stay with Robert and his crowd of locals and ex-pats. They would go to Wenceslas Square at midnight and drink champagne and vodka.

For Christmas, she bought him a fountain pen. She gave it to him one morning, as she was leaving his flat. It was still in the bag from the shop. He looked at it, disbelieving.

A fountain pen?

A ballpoint, at least, might have been useful for taking notes. His handwriting had always been rotten, and, having learned typing and shorthand, he could barely write longhand anymore.

That's a very nice pen, she said. He could see her getting angry, but he couldn't help himself.

What would a reporter do with a fountain pen?

Whatever you like, she said, and left.

On the one hand, he thought, twenty-seven years later, he had been very petty. On the other hand, it was not a very imaginative gift.

Was it that, or was it something else that had set her off, walking down the street in Prague, a day or two into their holiday, when, as they bickered on some minor point, something so trivial that, even a week later, he couldn't remember what it was – or more likely, didn't want to – she had turned to him and said, That's it. I'm sick of this. This is over.

And he had realised, stunned, that she really seemed to mean it.

Seriously? Couldn't this wait until we get home?

He went to the airline office to bring forward his return flight. When she heard he was changing his flight she got angry again, and accused him of sulking. Which, of course, he was. She didn't seem to understand why he was upset and wanted to cut short his time in her company. Maybe he'd misread her, escalated the situation, instead of biding his time until she calmed down. She was impulsive. That's what people still said about her, all these years later.

For years, he hadn't really thought about that journey home

from Prague. He had flown at night, alone. The plane stopped at Luxembourg, where they de-iced the wings. It landed at Shannon in the small hours, and he'd driven home to Dublin along the old N7, with its single lane and its sleeping towns, still years away from being bypassed. He thought he remembered moonlight and frost. He had passed a mile from the house he'd grown up in. It had been, he remembered now, for the first time in decades, a very sad drive.

Of course there had been unfinished business between them. But after that spectacular break-up, witnessed close-up by a bunch of their friends, you could never go back to how things had been. You had to commit to the roles that you'd taken. You couldn't spoil a good story like that. So when they met, after Prague, it was furtive and infrequent. He no longer went to her house and talked with her parents and siblings. She no longer came to his flat, which he shared with his brother. Instead, when they stayed together, it was at her new flat in Rathgar. And it was always Charlotte who took the initiative. He held himself back, because though he still wanted her, he would always resent her, and he was frightened of what she might do.

Their last time together was a year after the first. He was asked to write a colour piece about a big event outside Dublin, and they gave him two tickets and a hotel room. She came with him for the jaunt. He looked up the date, now, online.

It had been her twenty-fifth birthday. There was only one double bed in the room, so it was assumed that they'd share it, but not that it would necessarily go any further than that. In the end, late at night, they had turned to each other. It was tired and gentle. A writer would say, elegiac. It was clear it would never happen again.

Two weeks after Charlotte died he flew to Edmonton, Alberta, where he had lived as a child, and where his mother had since returned.

He knew, from previous experience, what would happen in Edmonton. The time difference would wake him in the dead hours of the morning, stuck in his mother's apartment. He hadn't had a good night's sleep in two weeks. To that would be added the time-shift of jet lag. He would have to find a way out of this trap.

Each morning, at two a.m., or four, he would get up, get dressed and sneak out of his mother's apartment in Garneau. He would walk across the High Level Bridge to the provincial legislature, turn and walk back on the other side of the bridge. He would do it twice, to put in roughly four miles, burning cigarettes like candles.

In the small hours of the morning, in February, from the High Level Bridge, Edmonton looks like a fairy-tale city:

the lights of downtown, the vapour from heating plants, the North Saskatchewan River, frozen over, except for a lead downstream from the bridge, open water steaming with frost. Black spruces in snow on the bluffs beneath the college.

There was a wire fence on the outside of the walkway that slanted inwards at the top, to stop people jumping off the bridge. Someone had attached laminated notices at the entrance to the walkway: *We need you here. You are filled with endless possibilities.*

He had a good winter coat. As he walked back and forth he talked with invisible people, people from the old days, and most of all with Charlotte. He saw fragments of sentences floating around him. Sometimes he stopped to take notes, which he typed into his phone, high above the frozen river. He thought, Maybe I'll get rid of this nonsense. Maybe I'll replace her with words.

But what, if anything, could he actually write, if he ever decided to write anything at all? It would be absurd to write a love letter to Charlotte, or a celebration, when she wasn't in his life and they had never been in love. Should he write something for all of them, for all of their people from then? But he was no longer in touch with them. And wasn't he too old to start having imaginary friends?

It came to him one morning, on the deserted bridge, two thirty a.m., minus twelve degrees Celsius, that he had fallen through a trapdoor into his twenties. This should have been obvious from the start. He had become, like Billy Pilgrim, spastic in time. The time-shift of jet lag only made this more stark. He didn't think that he had ever really been in love with Charlotte McDonald, except, of course, when they were lying together. But now that she was dead, his twenty-six-year-old self had escaped from inside him and was doing what he would have done had she died then, on her twenty-fifth birthday: he had fallen in love with some notions of her.

It was that simple, and that stupid. Because Charlotte McDonald hadn't died at the age of twenty-five. She had lived another twenty-six years, had a loving marriage, a glowing career, kids. She had told her own people, shortly before she died, that she'd had a great life, and she was always a straight-talker. And if a genie had appeared to them, in that guest-house mirror in Donegal, all those years ago, when they were so hot in their lives, and said, Listen, you can each have another twenty-six years, guaranteed – separate or together, that's up to you, but you're totally unsuited and you're too young to settle – and then die in the middle of everything, with all the big boxes ticked, surrounded by love; or you can turn down my offer, take your own chances, maybe die earlier, maybe lonely, maybe miserable, a failure in your own eyes, or maybe live on for much longer, long years of decline, watching your friends die, your own children grow old and slow and tired – wouldn't they both have grabbed at that deal?

And you'll slide around in time. Back and forth. And that's how he'd tell the story, if he ever decided to tell it.

His mother had recently had surgery and couldn't drive, so every day he took her out shopping in the Strathcona district. She had a Camry hybrid that she'd bought because she wanted to save the planet for his daughters, her only grandchildren. In London Drugs, she bought him a fancy infrared thermometer for the looming pandemic, but the hand sanitiser had already sold out. Then later, in Mark's Work Wearhouse, she found a stash of sanitiser, forgotten in a corner, and bought the whole box for him to take back to his people.

He took out the trash for her several times a day, an excuse to sneak a cigarette out by the dumpster, and he listened to the childhood wheeze and gurgle that had returned to his lungs, felt the old nicotine tremble, and he thought, So this is self-harming. How very dramatic. If that virus got into his lungs, the state he was in, he'd be finished. He'd be turning his face to the wall.

He had set up a file on his laptop computer, to prosecute his sins of omission. Charlotte was only one of many old friends that he'd meant to keep up with and had let slip away. This, it turned out, had been careless. Had he kept in touch, he'd have known that she was dying. He was being punished for that now. And he was also being punished for having so successfully hidden from himself the fact that he must have been at least a little in love with her, once, and that every time he had seen her again, at lengthening intervals down the years, it had still hurt, just a little, though she'd always been kind to him. Now, she would never hear a word from him again, but he was very much hearing from her.

He retrieved emails and texts, his fragments of memory. An obituary mentioned something that he had forgotten, or chosen to ignore. In it, a childhood friend said that Charlotte, despite her brash persona, had really been very shy. He had missed that. And it made perfect sense. She had shown the world a mask, and he had chosen not to notice. But he remembered now, too late, the way she had looked sometimes, when they were in company and she didn't know that he was watching her: self-conscious, frowning, slightly tense, as if she, like him, was holding it together. It had suited him then not to reach for that hidden person, to stay in his own armour, where he felt safe, rather than search for her depth. They might have been more alike than he'd imagined. But he now had no right to pretend to have known her at all.

★

Very early one morning in Edmonton, he came back from the High Level Bridge and got ready to shave and to shower. His hand shook as it held the razor, from nicotine and sleeplessness. And it came back to him then, looking in the mirror, that, for a while, after Donegal, he'd made an effort to shave the way that she'd told him. He thought, Is there anything left of Charlotte in the way I shave now?

He watched himself do it, hoping, but at the same time trying not to skew the experiment.

No. He had to be honest. He really couldn't see it. He must have slowly regressed to his old bad habits, lots of short, quick, uneven strokes, with and against the grain. Which was OK with the newer, better razors they make now that shave you closer than the old ones, with less risk of nicking yourself. The ones they had then would slice you to bacon. He no longer needed her help.

But how many times since then, after he put on the shaving cream, as he got ready to make the first pass with the razor, starting, as always, on his upper right cheek, how many times had he thought, for a moment, of Charlotte McDonald, offering unwanted advice in a Donegal guest house, bouncing up in the bed, the two of them bickering, still delighted with each other, her happy laugh and her chin raw from beard rash? How many thousands of times had he inwardly smiled at this memory, just for an instant, before he got on with his shave?

29

That moment was his. He alone had that of Charlotte. It was a funny story, too. And even if he was really just going through a load of self-indulgent middle-aged bollocks – which he was – if one side effect of this was to preserve a spark of someone good and true who had been in his life once, however briefly, whoever she really was, however unknowable now, wasn't that also something true and good?

He tried shaving her way, for old time's sake, then he gave up; it didn't feel right.

At the airport, he smoked three Du Mauriers in a row outside the terminal, until his lungs were screaming at him, then he binned the rest of the packet and went to board his plane.

One Friday afternoon, back in Dublin, just before the lockdown tightened, he drove Eleven out to Dollymount Strand for a walk. She liked to borrow his phone and play music through the car's speakers. Lately, by some kind of emotional osmosis, she had become fixated on two songs about death and failed connections: 'Ceremony', by New Order, and 'Tomorrow', by Ladytron.

This is why events unnerve me, they find it all, a different story . . .

I don't hate you, or want you, enough to wake you . . .

He asked her why she kept playing those songs. She said she liked the tunes.

They drove on to Bull Island via the causeway, parked near the roundabout, made their way on to the beach and turned north, into a cold wind. The beach was almost deserted, only the usual joggers and dog-walkers, businesslike people, pounding the sand.

They walked mostly in silence. The sky over Howth, normally a constellation of lights on a Friday evening, planes lined up like beads on final approach, was washed out and bare. Did he ever look at Howth without thinking, momentarily, of another old friend, who had grown up there?

When they reached the tip of the island, at Sutton Creek, they turned back. Dublin city and bay were spread before them. Ships thudded in and out of the port. He had come to this beach so often, when his children were smaller and his wife was at work. There was a big dune near the causeway, hidden away from the beach, that they called, among themselves, the Magic Mountain. The girls would charge down it towards him and he would catch them and throw them up in the air and catch them again. Or they played hide and seek – Be a monster, Dad! Be a monster! – and dug trenches with their plastic spades. On sunnier days, the children would play in the water, and he would watch them from a blanket on the beach, reading a book, knowing that they would have to wade a very long way before they were out of their depth. Then, as they got older, they would go further and further out, towards the point where the breakers calved from the greasy swell, and he'd have to wade out himself, hundreds of yards, until they could hear him shouting at them over the sound of the sea and the wind and the ships: Come back, you've gone too far.

This was his family's beach. His place. Beyond the isthmus of Sutton was the hump of Lambay Island. Charlotte said she had gone there once, with her first real boyfriend, who had some connection to the rich man who owned it. Lambay was across the sea from Malahide, where Charlotte had grown up, and where she had lain dying. That was her place. Only a few miles across the water, but a long way in time. It was how it should be.

He was a runner, though a heavy one, a plodder. He liked to run on this beach. He would plod on for a while longer. Charlotte, it turned out, would now always be a swimmer. In her final weeks, her people said, after the funeral, she'd been dreaming of the sea. How had it been, the last time she swam there? And had she known then that it was the last time? He saw her dive into the water, curving upwards again, towards the mirror of light where the waves meet the air. She had fooled him from the start. There was her depth. There was the biggest of ponds, just for her. She was tiny and weightless, undecided, looking up at the sky from under the sea.

March

Good Morning, Doctor Chandra

Simon had customised his Nokia so that, when you switched it on, a welcome note appeared on the screen. It said, *Good Morning, Doctor Chandra*.

The joke referred to the movie *2001: A Space Odyssey* and its sequel, *2010: The Year We Make Contact*, in which the sentient supercomputer, HAL, malfunctions and murders most of the crew of its spaceship. Growing up, Simon had always liked science fiction. They all had.

In the first film, HAL is shut down – killed – by the sole surviving crewman. In the sequel, a relief crew reaches the abandoned, drifting spaceship, and HAL's original programmer, Doctor Chandra, goes on board to reboot his creation. Back online, the computer speaks to its human father:

Good morning, Doctor Chandra. This is HAL. I'm ready for my first lesson.

Unlike *2001*, the sequel *2010* wasn't directed by Stanley Kubrick, and fewer people have seen it. Its emotional arc is completed when HAL achieves redemption – more than that, some form of eternal salvation – by sacrificing itself in a second death. But is it really HAL who dies, the second time around? You can reboot a computer, but can a mind return from the dead? Surely the real HAL, the HAL who went mad and murdered its shipmates, died in the first movie, on the last, slurred note of the song it was taught in early programming sessions, and that it sings again to astronaut David Bowman, its killer, and also its last witness, as it regresses to infancy and beyond, to the point where consciousness flickers and fades:

You'd look sweet . . . upon the seat . . . of a bicycle . . . made . . . for . . . two.

And yet, thanks to technology, Simon did survive death for a while, in a way. His phone message – Hi. Sorry I'm not on right now. Please leave a message, time and contact number, and I'll be back in touch with you – recorded in his deep, distracted voice, lingered for some time before his pay-as-you-go account ran out of credit and was, like HAL, deactivated. During that time, his eldest brother would still ring the number, to hear Simon's voice. He even topped up the credit, to keep that voice alive for a little while longer. But he had to let it go in the end. It wasn't really helping. Every few years, though, he would take the old phone out of the drawer, find an obsolete charger and power it up to see if it was working. And the welcome note would flash up on the screen:

Good Morning, Doctor Chandra.

Until that one afternoon in March, twenty years later, when he plugged in the phone and it wouldn't take a charge. And that was the end of it.

Some of Simon's other words also survived his death. A few of them were published in a book. A dozen years after Simon's death, when his eldest brother needed a suicide note for a character in his next novel, he decided to recycle one of a number of handwritten texts that he'd found in Simon's flat. There were several candidates among the hundreds of scribbles – wish lists, unsent and unrequited love letters, journal entries, reasons to be cheerful, motivational urgings, outpourings of self-loathing and despair – that had littered Simon's flat in Kildare Town. Simon seemed to have pushed himself to the brink of suicide several times, backed away again, but left the older notes lying about, uncancelled.

To know which note was the one that Simon had acted upon, the last in the series, his eldest brother would have had to have seen where the note had been left; the most recent, you'd think, would be the most prominent. It should have been easy to tell; the flat where Simon had died had to be cleaned and returned to the landlord, and the family had agreed that they would all meet a few days after the funeral, so they could do it together. But when Simon's eldest brother arrived at the appointed time, along with the middle brother, they found that their mother and sister had arrived earlier, and had already picked up all the papers, to tidy them. There was now no way to reconstruct their original placement. No way to establish a timeline.

To save something from the debris, the eldest brother decided to gather all these papers together and transcribe the most coherent and relevant fragments on to his laptop. He had been trained how to touch-type. He considered this a gift.

There were 4,284 words in the resulting .doc file, a rough edit of the last ten years of Simon's life. The stand-out candidate for best suicide note was this:

When you hold this note please don't be angry or sad. I'll sleep on it tonight – I always have before – the lure of a warm sleep. I know it's selfish. I'm sorry – it's been a long time coming but the notion has come calling many times before. I can't imagine moving forward in life and for as long as I can remember I haven't been able to. There have been pipe dreams which offered an imaginative buzz from time to time but they don't translate to reality. When that's a state of being with no avenues out, best to close the chapter.

Sixteen years later, these words were published in his eldest brother's third novel, reassigned to a fictional character who lived in the Canadian high Arctic. Simon had fantasised about this region in his notes to himself. He seemed to see it, paradoxically, as a place of warmth and refuge, where he could be alone, unjudged, no longer a failure in anyone's eyes, and especially not his own.

I may, however, have some real life ahead of me. Alaska through the mountains – set up where you can dog-sled into Alaska from the Canadian side in the heart of winter. Build igloos and sleep with dogs for warmth. VHF/short wave for communication. Grow a beard. Night-lights. Allsorts.

This note also went into the novel. The eldest brother thought that if he could smuggle some of Simon's words out into the world, even in disguise, they might keep him around for a little while longer.

Please don't be angry or sad. Night-lights. Good morning, Doctor Chandra.

Their father also came to the apartment to help clear up the mess. It was only the second time since their separation, nearly twenty years before, that their mother and father were required to spend time together, to cooperate, to acknowledge each other's existence. The previous time was at the funeral, a few days before. Now here they were again, in the small flat on the edge of the town, across the road from the school where Simon had begun his education. It was a decent flat, but Simon had trashed it. One of his great horrors, according to his private writings, was that people would see how he lived. They were seeing it now.

There was a lot of cleaning and tidying to do. As well as all the scraps of notes and scattered journals, there were dishes, bits of electronics, stale food, ashtrays overflowing with cigarette butts and roaches, empty beer cans, clothes, heaps of magazines and books and drawings. The work kept them all busy, too busy to feel any worse than they were feeling already. This had to be done, today, to get it over with, and they couldn't ask anyone else to do it for them. This, at last, was real family business. When everything else was done, their father, who ran his own construction business, went out to his truck and fetched a Stanley knife, which the eldest son used to cut a section of carpet from the middle of the bedroom, where the blood had pooled. And when he cut through the underlay, down to the bare concrete, some of the blood there was still red and wet, though it had been over a week since Simon had shed it. It looked like it was still alive.

★

On 7 May 1988 the Cill Dara under-eighteen rugby team played in the final of the Culliton Cup, at Landsdowne Road, in Dublin. They defeated Dundalk by thirteen points to six. The big stadium was crowded, because the under-eighteen game was a curtain-raiser for a much bigger match, the Leinster Senior Cup final between Blackrock and Trinity.

Simon was, unlike either of his brothers, a natural athlete and sportsman, even though he was never that bothered about sports. Six foot three, rangy, naturally fit until the end of his life, he played in second row that day. Cill Dara, a relatively new club from a small provincial town, hadn't had much success up to then. This was a long way from the moneyed world of private-school rugby, but it was a big deal for the town, and a lot of people came to Lansdowne who probably hadn't been there before to watch rugby – Gaelic football supporters from Round Towers, and Ellistown, and Rathangan. Most of Simon's family was there too, in the west stand, on their feet, euphoric. Simon was winning. That was the day that Simon was a hero, and could still see past the clouds that were gathering around him.

There were other hopeful signs for him, around that same time. The middle brother had taken up cycling, and Simon tried his hand at it too. His first race was a local event, but the field was full of seasoned racers, grown men who rode scores of miles every week. Simon won it, then won a couple more. Then he no longer bothered.

He'd never played Gaelic football – their local all-boys Catholic school, small and almost heroically threadbare, didn't have a football team, or any other kind of organised sports – but, one weekend, Simon was persuaded to make up the numbers for Monasterevin, at the last minute. After that, they would send cars to the house on Sunday mornings, trying to persuade him to get out of bed. But it was also in this period that Simon would fail his school Leaving Certificate, despite having been, as baffled teachers kept telling his mother, one of the brightest boys in the school. The family couldn't understand it. Simon could have got a pass, even a few honours, with very little study. Really, he just had to turn up and concentrate for the three hours of each exam. And Simon couldn't understand it either, how he couldn't do something that looked so simple, even to him. Interrogated by his family, he would sit there, mumbling, snatching at phrases – I don't know . . . It's just that . . . – and a look would come into his eyes, as if a shadow had fallen behind them, between him and the world, and he would shake his head to clear it, but it wouldn't go away.

Simon was skilled at drawing, and his mother helped him to send a portfolio to the school of art at Oxford Polytechnic, which didn't care about Leaving Cert results. He was offered a place, provided he finished a foundation course in Harrow, west London. It seemed to start well, but then he stopped showing up for his classes. The college alerted his mother. Simon couldn't be found. They called friends of his eldest brother, people from the town who now lived in Finsbury Park, and they went and found him. He had suffered some sort of breakdown, or maybe that's not the word, maybe 'stoppage' would do it. Depression, bipolar, whatever, there never seemed to be a settled diagnosis, or meds that really worked. But it was fair to say that Simon had suffered the first of his stoppages. He was smoking too much cannabis, which was a cause, or a symptom, or both. He never moved on to harder drugs, but, as it turned out, the light ones were still too heavy for him.

They brought him back from London, back to the house in the country, five miles outside town, where – the rest of the family having by then scattered to Dublin, England, Canada – he lived alone with his sister. His father, who now lived on the other side of the county, was desperate to help him, and gave him work in his construction business, which provided specialist services, mainly to horse farms. Simon started out well again, then began to have more stoppages. He wouldn't turn up for work, or would pick fights with the foreman in front of the other workers. You can't run a business that way. His father, an alcoholic who'd been sober for decades, had offered advice that he'd learned himself the hard way, had fed and clothed Simon, put him up when he had to, and had given him his own van to drive, but he had no choice but to let him go.

Simon moved up to Dublin. His eldest brother, who was in a slump then too, let him sleep on the floor of his freezing Fairview bedsit. A friend of the eldest brother's sort-of ex, who ran a chain of pizzerias, gave him a job delivering pizza on his eldest brother's bicycle. That worked for a while, until a car hit Simon, injuring him slightly, and he began to talk of the big compensation claim that would solve all his problems, set him up for the future. He stopped showing up to deliver the pizza. By now, his brother no longer wanted to ask why. He had problems of his own with untreated depression, and he was embarrassed by Simon. The bicycle was stolen or lost.

In 1992, Simon made the first of three attempts to kill himself. He swallowed a large quantity of paracetamol pills, and ended up in the emergency room, and then St John of God's psychiatric hospital in Stillorgan. As it happened, they had all been to St John of God's before, when they were children, to visit their father. They were told, back then, that their father had an illness called alcoholism, and that the hospital would treat him. It all sounded very proper and settled, and the four children had accepted this information with solemn approval. Of course the hospital would sort out whatever was wrong with their father. (What was wrong with their father, anyway? It was mostly kept from the kids.) The hospital was a very nice place. It had its own sweet shop, and landscaped grounds that they could play in, while their mother, her face tight with worry, talked tersely with their father, both of them controlling their voices, so the other guests and patients in the room wouldn't hear.

Now, fifteen years later, when Simon became a patient himself, the hospital was even nicer. You sat at tables or on couches in the communal central area, its big picture windows looking on to those same grounds, and you waited there while your loved one was called from their ward, and you gave them whatever you'd brought them – the biscuits, money, books and cigarettes – and you sat there and drank weak coffee, eating some of the biscuits, but you still controlled your voices so that others wouldn't hear.

Visiting hours were in the early evening. It amazed the eldest brother, only a few years later, how crass he had been about his brother's situation. He'd made Simon sit there and listen while he fumbled about stupidly, looking for explanations, advice, diagnoses, facile zen-like cures. Life isn't so bad. Why not just try harder? It isn't that hard, if you try. We'll help you, when you get out of here. We'll do everything we can. And Simon had sat there, smiling politely, with the shadow behind his eyes.

The thing about Simon was, everyone loved him. The gentle giant, they called him in the town. He was the heart of any party, when he wasn't in a hole, and when he was in a hole then people didn't see him. When he was in a hole he would 'go nocturnal', as he put it in his writings: sleep by day, then come alive at night – if you could call it living – smoking hash and drinking alcohol, if he could afford them, dodging the landlord, dreading any meeting with anyone he knew. Sometimes, he was too paralysed even to sign on for his dole. Sometimes, he starved. But he was never deluded, unfortunately. He knew what he was doing. He wrote it all down.

In between times, though, on his good days, he had a big, clear singing voice, and could hold his own in any session. He was funny, and well read, and good looking. He never had any problem attracting women, though keeping them was another thing, the way that he lived. There was a lot about that in his writing.

On New Year's Eve 1999, Simon was not in a hole. He'd spent Christmas in Dublin, in the Donnybrook house which their mother, who had come back for the holidays from her new home in Alberta, had rented so they could spend Christmas together – the house in Kildare having since been sold. On Christmas night, he and his eldest brother sat up late watching *It's a Wonderful Life*, a film that neither had seen before, or would ever watch again.

Things were looking up for Simon. His mother had made a big effort to lift him out of his holes. His bills had been paid for him, and he was enrolled on a sculpting and bronze casting course, which he thought might be his way out. His mother had also paid to have his teeth done; they'd been a cause of pain and embarrassment to him for a while. Everyone had given Simon nice and useful presents, and also money. So, on 31 December 1999, the biggest New Year's Eve in a thousand years, Simon had left his flat and gone up the town, to the Silken Thomas, where he'd had a great evening with lots of old friends.

He went there again the following night. His eldest brother, who was having a quieter night in Dublin, got a call from Simon some time before midnight, the first day of the new millennium. Simon sounded happy and calm, almost serene. They talked for a while about who had been around the old town for the celebrations, who had come back from where. His eldest brother regretted that he hadn't gone back there that year. It would have been nice to see the old faces. But where would he have stayed? The family no longer had a home in Kildare. There was no question of him staying with Simon, whose current flat he'd never even seen. They wished each other good night, and a happy new year.

A couple of days later, Simon's eldest brother flew back to Johannesburg, where he then lived. He was sitting at the table where he worked, in the dining room of his one-bedroom mine house in Melville, when the telephone rang. His father started to speak, and then he broke down.

It's Simon, he finally managed to say.

He asked his son to tell Simon's mother. He said he couldn't bring himself to do it. So Simon's eldest brother called his mother in Grande Prairie, Alberta, where she had just returned after the holidays. Even a few days later, he couldn't remember a word of that call.

In the taxi on the way to Johannesburg airport, to catch his second flight home within a month, he called a friend in Cape Town. She was the partner of a veteran correspondent who'd shown him the ropes when he first arrived in Africa, and she had invited him to stay with them at the Cape, starting that weekend. He leaned away from the driver, lowered his voice, so the driver wouldn't hear him. He found his situation delicate, even embarrassing.

I'm sorry, he told her. I can't come to Cape Town after all. There's been a death in my family.

What?

She barked out the question. She couldn't hear him. He raised his voice a little.

It's my brother. He shot himself.

What?

It occurred to him that she was more deaf than she cared to admit. He had to shout.

I can't come to Cape Town. My brother has shot himself.

She heard him that time. She was, of course, very shocked and sympathetic. They ended the call.

After a minute or two, the driver, a Serbian immigrant, cleared his throat carefully, his eyes still on the road.

I'm sorry, he said.

Because they no longer had a family house in which to lay Simon out, he had to lie in a funeral home beside the flat he'd died in – the funeral home belonged, in fact, to Simon's landlord. That's how small towns work.

Simon had been a laughing child, but as he got older his face set into a frown. He was frowning now. There was a bruise on his forehead, just over the right eye, and a discolouration, like the stain left by iodine. His eldest brother wondered if this was a sign of haemorrhage, or a skilfully concealed exit wound. Had he put the barrel in his mouth, or under his chin? He was wearing a woollen turtleneck sweater that he would never have worn in life. It hid his neck right up to the chin. So maybe that's where the damage was done. Or perhaps there were scars on his throat from the autopsy. It didn't really matter, except that Simon would have hated that sweater. When he kissed Simon's forehead it tasted of chemicals, and it was very cold. So this is what love means, he thought.

The priest at the funeral was not one of the regular priests from the parish. He was an old schoolmate of their father. His sermon wasn't really a sermon, or a eulogy; it was more of a talk about life and love and what we don't know about them, all of that, with almost nothing at all about God. Simon's eldest brother thought it was very good, though he couldn't remember a word of it later. He himself had to give a reading from the Bible, from the alter, and managed to get through it without breaking down. Fortunately, he had a line from the TV comedy *Father Ted* stuck in his head, one from the episode where the alcoholic Father Jack dies after drinking floor polish, and Father Ted and Father Dougal have to sit vigil with his corpse in the chapel, and, in the middle of the night, Father Ted starts philosophising about death, sitting beside the coffin, quoting verbatim from Joyce's 'The Dead', and Father Dougal chimes in, That's very morbid, isn't it, Ted? What started you off thinking about death?

In the church, on the alter, he kept hearing Simon saying that phrase. That's very morbid, isn't it? It almost made him laugh.

Their father's family had been in the county for a long time, and had many other branches, and Simon was also well liked in the town. So the parish church was packed for the funeral. There were even a couple of people that Simon had known in St John of God's, pale young women who would sometimes come and sit with Simon and his eldest brother, pooling their quiet dismay. Many of the eldest brother's friends came down from Dublin, even though most of them hadn't known Simon, because in Ireland you don't just go to funerals for the dead, you go for the survivors, to show that you're still there. The Finsbury Park contingent came back from London. People like that.

Because the family had no place of its own to wake Simon, it had hired the function room of the Silken Thomas, where Simon had spent, as far as anyone knew, his last two good nights on earth. People kept coming up to Simon's eldest brother, shaking his hand, telling him their stories about Simon in the good times, which he very much wanted to hear. Many of them also told him about the last time they'd seen Simon alive, as if that was important to them, as if the eldest brother wasn't the only one who cared about time-lines. A few of them said they'd seen Simon ambling across the diamond in front of the church, on his way up the town from his flat, days after he'd probably already killed himself. His eldest brother didn't bother to correct them. Who was he to say they weren't telling the truth, or to deprive Simon of another day or two of life?

A few people asked the eldest brother that day, and others would ask at intervals thereafter, until the whole business had faded, if he was angry with Simon for what he had done. And he said no. He was never angry for a second. Simon had been suffering. He had fought very hard, and it hadn't worked out for him. He had no dependants, and he had a right to make his own decision. It was just very sad, that's all.

No one knew how long Simon had lain on the carpet in the middle of the bedroom. The date of death was given as 7 January 2000, but that was really just the day he was found. The family heard that the medical examiner thought he'd died several days earlier. Probably on the night of New Year's Day, which was the last time anyone had definitely heard from him. When Simon had called his eldest brother that night, for an idle chat, he'd been secretly saying goodbye.

The flat was unheated, and the weather was cold, so it really hadn't made a whole lot of difference how long he'd lain there. Anyway, all these questions were smoothed over at the inquest in Naas's beautiful courthouse. The toxicology report said that there was nothing improper in his system, which seemed unlikely, given how long cannabis can linger in the blood. But they probably let stuff like that slide, back then, for the sake of the family. This was rural Ireland, and the cause of death was obvious. The coroner offered his condolences to the family, and thanked them for their patience. Did they have any questions? No, they did not.

Apart from the verdict, there was also a recommendation that their second cousin, who had illegally loaned Simon his licensed .22 rifle, should have his gun confiscated. The cousin had to appear as a witness. Afterwards, outside the courthouse, Simon's family shook the cousin's hand and told him they knew it wasn't his fault. They were country people. Young lads sometimes lent each other licensed hunting guns, without worrying too much about the letter of the law. They told him they were sorry that he would have to lose his rifle, though they could tell he never wanted to see it again.

Twenty years and several weeks after Simon's death, the midterm holidays came around again. It was wet and cold, and all the usual fun parks and activities were still closed for the winter, so Simon's eldest brother decided to take his two Dublin-born girls down to Kildare, to do the guided tour of the Irish National Stud. He'd never done that tour himself, though he used to sneak into the stud with his friends when he was the girls' age. After the guided tour, they would visit his aunt in the townland of Oghill – *Eo choill*, the yew wood – where he'd grown up. The girls hadn't seen their aunt for ages, and he'd recently been reminded how important it was to keep in touch. Plus, with his wife at work, it would get them all out of the house for a day. There was talk of a lockdown, so it would be good to see the countryside while they could.

The tour was very interesting, though it drizzled the whole time. After it was over, they had lunch in the cafe, but there were still two hours to kill until it was time to visit his aunt. He suggested going to Donnelly's Hollow, but his daughters, too old for that now, wanted to drive in the warm car while they listened to music – Thirteen on her headphones, Eleven on her father's phone, via the car's Bluetooth speakers. 'Ceremony', by New Order. 'Tomorrow', by Ladytron.

So that's what they did. Leaving the National Stud, their father turned on to the road from Tully to Newtown, and then, on a whim, diverted down the boreen to St Brigid's Well. He hadn't been down that lane in thirty years, but this was Brigid's parish, and her feast day had been only a few weeks before. One of his old school friends used to live by the well, in a house that belonged to the National Stud. He'd often get his tea there, when he was twelve, and sometimes stayed over. He wanted to see that friendly house again. But he saw now that it had become derelict, with bushes growing through the roof. The holy well, once a dignified pattern of rushes and water and simple old stones, had been tarted up with gimcrack shrines and fairy trees covered in ribbons, a tradition unknown in Kildare when he was a kid, but which had clearly since been imported, from the west or the south, or the pages of a book.

They drove through Kildare Town, took the old N7 to Cherryville Cross, turned right. The kids were oblivious. They were city born and raised. They didn't care where they were. He hadn't driven this road in almost thirty years, and took a wrong turning before finding his way to Rathangan. At the end of the main street of that charming little village, he showed them its titular *rath*, or Iron Age earthen fort, and told them how it had once been the capital of the ancient kingdom of Uí Failghe, or Offaly, but was now deep inside County Kildare.

Deal with it, BIFFOs, he said, which got a laugh from his daughters, who knew that Offaly was now the name of a neighbouring, rival county, and that BIFF stood for Big Ignorant Fucker From. But he also got a laugh when he added, All your base are belong to us – an old computer-game reference that they couldn't possibly have got. They were humouring him.

From Rathangan they took the road to Monasterevin – a road which, he remembered, Simon had driven late at night, in a truck with their cousins, who liked to fire shotguns at the road signs as they sped past. Music playing, they drove past Moore Abbey, where Gerard Manley Hopkins had been particularly miserable, and on south through Kildangan, towards Kilberry. They were now in the low, swampy country of Kildare's western border, the valley of the River Barrow, a place of rushes and bog ash and shuttered-up houses, a cold Louisiana. He was planning to show his children the Cush Inn, where his mother's father, who'd lived with them, and to whom he'd been close, in the quiet way of that time, would sometimes go for an afternoon pint, treating his eldest grandson to crisps and lemonade. He remembered that the Cush, an Irish take on a honky-tonk roadhouse, used to have a plastic Elvis outside it, one arm raised, triumphant, mid jive. He thought that his jackeen daughters would think this was funny. But the Cush Inn was gone, completely levelled, replaced by a plant that made gas out of pig shit. He wondered what had happened to the plastic Elvis. He hoped that it hadn't gone into a skip.

They backtracked to Kildangan, turned right at Boland's

Cross, went through the village and past Kildangan Stud, where Simon had worked on a job for their father, and where, decades before, the artist Francis Bacon spent part of his boyhood, about as happily as you'd expect. They drove past the thatched cottage – a rarity in those parts – where, they'd been warned as children, a writer lived, though no one knew his name, or what he wrote. The house still seemed to be inhabited, but the thatch was beginning to rot. In Oghill, he pulled up outside the house he'd grown up in, the house his family had built for themselves when they moved here from Canada, on a plot gifted to them by their father's kind brother. The new owners had made some improvements to the house, which he pointed out to his daughters, who didn't care.

You should drive on, they said, before someone looks out and sees us. They'll think that we're weird.

And so up the road, to tea and biscuits at his aunt's house. She was as cheerful as always, which, on a day so bleak that it was almost funny, was a very good thing. The children were perfectly happy. They liked listening to music as they drove around. They liked chocolate biscuits, and they liked their great aunt, whom they didn't see often enough. None of this other stuff mattered to them. And they hadn't noticed when, after they drove past Moore Abbey, on the edge of Monaster-evin, their father had slowed the car and started to inch right, across the white dividing line, towards the entrance to the graveyard on the side of Kill Hill. They hadn't noticed, either, when he'd changed his mind, straightened the wheel again, put his foot on the pedal and drove on without stopping. This was the place, but it wasn't the time. This was no time to tell his daughters that they should have had another uncle, one who had stopped his own clock three weeks short of his thirtieth birthday, whom they would never meet, and whose name they had never heard spoken. This was no time to tell them that Simon would have been a good uncle. He was very fond of small children and animals. He was always looking for things to look after, being unable to look after himself.

Some other time. Until then, Simon would stay in the family silence.

His mother and father had, separately, done everything they could for Simon. They had paid for treatments, found him apartments, got him jobs, fed him, put him up on occasion, enrolled him in courses. They had visited him in hospital, and loved him. The summer before he died, their mother had paid for Simon to fly to Alberta, where she now lived, and where the middle brother had just moved with his new wife. The eldest brother had taken leave from Africa to join them there, and, on a jaunt paid for by their mother, all three brothers had driven together from Grande

Prairie to Edmonton, where they'd lived as small children. In Edmonton, they spent a night in a series of bars. It was, in fact, the first time that all three of them had ever gone drinking together – and, as it turned out, the last. Which was a pity, because it also turned out they worked well as a crew. The following morning, badly hungover, they went to look at the house they'd lived in as children. The eldest brother, who was the only one old enough to have any clear memory of it, said he didn't recognise it. He didn't think it was the right one. But that was the address their mother had given them. She said she was pretty sure.

After that, they drove west to Jasper, then south through the Rockies. The eldest brother had given Simon a second-hand camera and lens, because Simon wanted to try his hand at photography. Unlike his eldest brother, he did have an eye. Having stopped in the mountains to look at a bear, Simon absent-mindedly left the camera on the roof of the car. As they drove off again, they saw it smashing on the tarmac in the rear-view mirror. That sort of thing often happened to Simon, in the war of attrition, of unsprung concentration that was his life. He was devastated, unable to talk or to look at his brothers. He'd already pinned big hopes on that camera. He was always looking for another way out.

Everyone had done everything they could. That's what you think, until it's too late, and all the other things that you could have done show up on your doorstep, presenting their bills. Maybe they could have done more for him. Maybe they could have understood him.

A strange thing happened after Simon's death. It was like his last joke. He began to work little miracles. Having lived for years on emotional islands, shying from all but polite encounters, the surviving members of the family began to make tentative contact. It was now or never. All of them could see that, though no one said it aloud. The silence was still there, but now at least they could see each other waving.

Their sister, who had been the most introverted of all of them, took on a new life. Having drifted from one postgraduate course to the next ever since college, she found one she was good at, began to assert herself, became an outspoken class rep, graduated top of her class. She got a good job on the back of it, and promotions, and thrived. She and her mother grew closer, went travelling, had fun. The strangest thing of all was that their sister began ending long-distance phone calls, which were now rather more frequent, by saying, with a mixture of determination and resignation, I love you. Sometimes, they'd admit that they loved her too.

The eldest brother had looked into the coffin in the funeral home and seen himself lying there. He had told himself that, if Simon was dead, it was now up to him to go on living for his brother, to keep Simon alive inside him until it was his turn to go. And he was forced to admit that he wasn't living well. The life he had in Africa, which was built on what he'd romanticised as adventure and freedom, but was in fact tunnel vision, the next drug or high, chasing other people's stories and not looking back, nor asking himself why he was doing it, or what it was for – this wasn't a life that he wanted anymore, though he'd given himself entirely to it, shedding good people as he went. He would have to find something better, while there was time.

Good Morning, Doctor Chandra. I'm ready for my first lesson.

For many years before Simon's death, the eldest brother had a recurring dream in which he was talking to his late grandfather, his mother's father, who had left Cavan for England in the Great Depression, and spent most of his life driving a black cab in Manchester. After he retired, he had lived with them in Kildare until he died, and had quietly kept the family going in the hard times, almost unnoticed. In this dream, they talked about day-to-day matters, and, as he was talking to his grandfather, he was both happy and troubled. It was nice to talk, but something was wrong, something he couldn't quite grasp, and as the conversation went on he would slowly begin to understand, at a different level of dream consciousness, that his grandfather was dead, had been dead for a long time, and yet here they were, talking. It was a sad dream, but a good one. Sometimes, he felt close to tears when he woke from it, but it was always good to have.

Their grandfather had died in the summer of 1988, at the age of seventy-eight, reading in his favourite chair, in the corner of the living room, where the afternoon sun shone, and from which you could see the wooded hump of Kill Hill, where he and Simon would be buried together. His eldest grandson had been in Toronto for the summer when his grandfather died, having just finished university, and he had to fly back for the funeral. Earlier that summer, just before he'd flown out to Canada, after his final exams, he and his grandfather had watched Ireland beat England in the group stage of the European football championship. They had hugged each other when Ray Houghton scored the winning goal, something they'd otherwise never have done, back then, as grown Irish males. Later that summer, his grandfather, a quiet, neat and deeply unselfish person, had stolen away, leaving no unfinished business.

Simon, on the other hand, had thrown a brick through the pane of his own life. There were pieces of him everywhere. He now took his grandfather's place in his brother's recurring dream. Afterwards, his brother could never remember what they'd talked about, or what they were doing, but he always remembered Simon's expression in the dream, how he listened to his eldest brother talking well-meaning non-sense, sometimes nodding, sometimes replying. He no longer had the shadow. Instead, there was a new look in Simon's eyes – sly, a little amused – the look of someone who knows something you don't, something funny, but that you'll find out soon enough. He was the eldest brother, now.

April

The Rain Queen

The children ask him if he's ever seen a ghost, and he thinks, That depends, but he tells them no, he doesn't think he has. And then he thinks some more, and he says, I don't think I've ever *seen* a ghost, but something ghostly happened to me once, twenty years ago, just before I left Johannesburg. And then he adds, I mean, I say it happened to *me,* but it actually happened to everyone on the Witwatersrand, along the Main Reef Road from Soweto to Benoni. So there were millions of witnesses, although a lot of them might not have noticed at the time. And it *was* very spooky.

Then, because they are all stuck at home in Dublin on what should be a school day, because of the virus, he tells them what happened when the Rain Queen died. And because they have so much time on their hands, he lays it on thick.

He tells them about Modjadji, the ruler and oracle of the Lobedu people, who live in the north of the Transvaal, in the escarpment above the Limpopo, in a land so old that forests of cycads, of dinosaur trees, linger in the warm, moist air rising up from the bushveld. He tells them that the Rain Queen was said to be immortal, and that mighty warriors and leaders – Shaka Zulu, Moshoeshoe the Great, P. W. Botha, Nelson Mandela – had sent her gifts and messengers, seeking her friendship and asking her to send rain for their crops, which was her great power. And he tells them how her mystery and magic had shielded her small, peaceful nation from the Zulus and Shangaan and Swazis and Boers. Until the night that she finally died.

The Rain Queen is dead, long live the Rain Queen. Because it was the Lobedu custom that every queen was reincarnated, on her death, in her appointed successor, who took on her name, Modjadji, so her rule could continue, immortal. But then the third century of her reign began, and with it our third millennium, and, when the fifth Modjadji died, there was no one to replace her, because her chosen heir, her own daughter, had herself died, very young, only two days before. The line was broken. There was no Rain Queen. And he tells his children how, as he was typing up this story for his newspaper, sitting at his kitchen table in Johannesburg (the one he'd been sitting at the year before, when his father had called to tell him about Simon), he'd heard a plink on the roof of the little tin-topped mine house, then another, and another, and the skies had opened and it started to rain.

His daughters look at him, expectant, because that can't be the point of the story; after all this build-up, there must be something more. So what if it rained? It rains all the time in Ireland. And he takes a beat, and then delivers the pay-off: it was midwinter when the Rain Queen died, and on South Africa's Highveld Plateau, it never, *ever* rains in midwinter. He tells them that not once in the seven southern winters that he spent in Johannesburg did he see a drop of rain in June or July. Except for the night that the Rain Queen died, when it came down in torrents.

The girls like this story very much. They might even believe it. And why shouldn't they? It's true.

But, telling it, it seems so neat. It seems like something that a writer would write. And because he has recently discovered that the past is no longer where he thought he'd left it, safely behind him, he feels a sudden need to re-examine his own tale, the one about the Rain Queen, even though it's one of those stories that are classed, in the trade, as too good to check. Did it really happen, the way he now remembers it? How good a job did he make of the piece that he remembers writing about it, twenty years before? He opens his laptop, selects the finder.

The thing is, he can't find any trace of the piece he wrote about the Rain Queen, if it ever even existed. He thought he'd kept most of the articles that he wrote in his old life, the original .doc files, stored on his hard drive, but now that he looks for them, they aren't there. They must have fallen through the cracks in some backup or upgrade. Then he looks for the story in the online archives of the papers that he used to write for, but still nothing shows. And he begins to wonder, not for the first time, about his absences of mind, and false memory syndrome.

According to the Internet, the fifth Rain Queen died at the time he remembers, in the southern midwinter of 2001. That was after he'd already told his bosses he was giving up that line of work (which turned out not to be true) and that he was leaving Africa (which was). For various reasons, he was living pretty badly at that time. Did the thing really happen the way he remembers it, or was it a dream, or – worse – a delusion?

And then, just when he is getting worried, he finds a link to a piece in the *New York Times*, dated 30 June 2001, by Donald G. McNeil Jr, a colleague whom he remembers well. This piece tells the same story that he told his kids, pretty much, and it has what American reporters call a kicker, a punchy last sentence, a sting in the tail.

Unseasonable rains hit Johannesburg on Thursday and continued this evening.

The fact remains, his memory has gaps in it, and some of those gaps may be strategically placed. He has a history of blanking major details of his life. And he wonders, How does anyone go through analysis? How can you tell the doctor how you feel about your life, when life itself is so hard to remember? Do people just end up making things up, or going with their best guesses, to tell themselves a story while the doctor checks their watch? For that kind of money, you have to come up with something. Everyone's a writer now.

Or maybe he's an exception to the general rule, having found in his own life so little worth remembering. If only for practical reasons, he should have established some means to hold himself to account. He should have kept a diary, even a superficial one. If he had, he could have turned it into some sort of book, the sort of book that reporters write. But to write that book, a non-fiction one, in the first person, he would have had to find a theme for it, and he would have had to be part of that theme. And he didn't interest himself enough to want to use himself as a character. So he stuck to the sugar rush of other people's stories, the ones he got paid for at the end of the month. He had felt proud that his work was expendable, which was true, and that so was he, which was self-romanticising bollocks. It doesn't matter, colleagues would say in the bar (there was usually a bar). By tomorrow night, your deathless prose will be wrapping someone else's fish and chips, mate. And all this was fine, no problem at all, just doing the job – until twenty years later, when his kids wanted a ghost story, and he realised, as he told it, that he was now one of its ghosts.

What did it amount to? What will he tell his kids, if they ever bother to ask any further? They don't take a lot of interest. They think he's always just been in the house, doing school runs and drop-offs, taking them to the beach or to sports, cooking bad dinners, typing in the box room, rodding blocked drains.

Did he cover the fall of apartheid? No, that was over when I got there. I reported on the transition . . . He wouldn't expect many follow-up questions about a *transition*. There was a terrible thing in Rwanda, but again, he was a few weeks too late to say, I was there. He did see the aftermath of Rwanda's Year Zero, and the bodies, and the rest of it, but that's not the kind of thing the cool people boast about. Much less to their kids. There was a man called Mobutu in a leopard-skin hat, and wars that are hard to explain now, and that never really ended. Debt. Colonialism. Corruption. Racism. Tribalism.

Diamonds, coltan and oil. Later, there was Israel and Palestine, which never changes, except that it always gets worse. Jerusalem, where the followers of three great religions fight over the same futile rocks.

There was good stuff too, the thousand acts of friendship and kindness from people who had little or nothing to give him and even less reason to give it. He remembers the protestors in Kinshasa, who rescued him from the police and brought him wet rags to wash tear gas from his eyes. You have to tell our story, they said, and he did that, as well as he could, but he didn't have the heart to tell them how little anyone on the outside would care, much less remember, a day or two later. Including himself, once he'd moved on to the next story. What were they even protesting about, exactly? Étienne Tshisekedi . . . He should go and look him up . . .

He remembers the important TV reporters, presenting pieces to camera on rooftops or high ground, while behind them the picturesque victims streamed past. These people have no hope, they'd declaim. He overheard several of them saying that phrase, always in the same tone of pious disappointment, even after it had become a cliché, an in-joke. If these people had no hope, what were they doing there, carrying their children and all the stuff they could drag with them, running from their old lives into the unknown? They were dead on their feet from the hope.

He remembers the little boys on the shore of Lake Albert, two in the morning, taking turns to run up and touch his arm through the open truck window, because they wanted to know if white people felt as cold as they looked. He remembers a gift of swamp rice with spicy peanut sauce, when he hadn't had a cooked meal for weeks. He remembers Captain Valentine Strasser in Paddy's Beach Bar, in Freetown, sitting sadly in the corner with his bodyguards, unable to join in the dancing, because Strasser was now the president of Sierra Leone, an office he'd attained by accident, legend had it, *primus inter pares* in a putsch by junior officers, through the fame he'd gained as a champion disco dancer. Another story that was too good to check.

Did you save anyone's life, Dad?

Kind of, once, but he probably died anyway.

Did your stories sell papers?

I don't know, but I got paid.

Did you ever get shot at?

Not very well.

Did you do any good?

Not that I can say.

Were there elephants?

Yes. There were elephants and gorillas and lions and crocodiles. There was the silence of the bush at sundown, and clouds in vast skies. There were acacia trees, and baobabs, and the bougainvillea bush at the door of the mine house. Hadeda ibises and Parktown prawns. Pretoria from the air, purple with jacaranda, and thunderstorms patrolling the Highveld at night. There were three-day drives to remote and lovely places, environmental stories, four-wheel-drive trucks, sleeping under the stars in deserts at night. There was the corniche in Beirut, and the palaces of Isfahan. Cheering crowds in fallen cities, free helicopter rides.

It sounds really great, his children might some day tell him. And he'd tell them, Yes, it was.

Kiley, whom he'd met on his second day in Africa, in Goma, put it best: I can't believe that I get paid to have adventures. They were drinking cold beer on the terrace of the Black and White Bar, in Bo, Sierra Leone, a few months after that meeting in Goma, watching a sudden evening shower scattering the people in the street. The hiss of the drops on tin roofs and tree leaves, the iron smell of the rain in dry soil. The people in the street laughed as they ran for cover. They needed this rain, but they hadn't expected it. Remember. There were also so many moments like that.

What he then cared about most was what he might see next, hoping that it might distract him from whoever he was, transform him into something more poetic, more weary and saddened and wise. He wanted to be like the people in the Greene and Conrad novels. Even more, he wanted to be accepted by the others, the ones who were already there when he arrived. And in this new life, the hierarchy was clear and, in its own way, meritocratic. There was a joke, often told pointedly: How many Sarajevo correspondents does it take to change a light bulb? You don't know? Of course you don't know. *You weren't there.*

He was too late for Bosnia, but he was still pretty lucky. His first big story, the Goma refugee crisis of 1994 – thousands of Rwandan refugees dying of cholera, corpses lining the road, for miles, north and west – was already something to boast about, only weeks later. Yes, I was there. Were you?

He would later beat that high, but he would never match the horror. He was winning from the start. He'd stood, that second day, in the livid green banana grove north of the city, sunlight red from the dust of the erupting volcano, and watched them swinging the bodies into the mass grave. One man took the hands, the other the feet. The bodies arced through the air from the back of the truck, and when they landed in the pile he heard dead limbs snapping, the comical coconut sound of skulls striking skulls. He saw the eyes of the young French soldier who was directing the bulldozer, stark above the mask that covered the rest of his face, and he knew it was true, what he'd read as a kid in his war books, that there is such a thing as a thousand-yard stare. But he also understood that he would never have to have one. The fact is, he was just passing through.

He'd stood in the lava dust outside the Red Cross tent and watched the refugees bring in their dying and dead, dozens of bodies lying heaped against the canvas, bulging it inwards, against the still-living bodies in the cots inside the tent, the lucky few who'd been triaged and were being rehydrated, who would rise from the dead within minutes. And he looked at the ground in front of him, where a family lay dying, a mother and her young children. She lay on her side, facing away from her children, drawing with her finger minute patterns in the dirt. Other refugees milled around them on dazed errands of their own. For a moment, she turned her sunken eyes and looked up at him, listless, incurious, then went back to whatever she saw in the dust. Years later, she would be the only one of the thousands that he could see in his memory. There was nothing he could do for her. She would never make it into that tent. He watched her dying, took some notes, maybe too many, and tried to remember not to chew on his pen. But he knew that, even if he did chew it to a stub, as was his habit, and he caught cholera from it, that some other white person would take him away and give him antibiotics. He'd be back to work in one or two days.

Dying of cholera wasn't for him. He was a glorified tourist, a species of travel writer. But he felt so exalted by all this living and dying, the African colours, the stink of the shit, the abandoned weapons heaped up at the border, and he knew he would never go back to any newsroom. He also knew that his excitement was shameful, and that bills would come due. Better to pay something down now, up front. So he decided to forge his own alibi. He decided – he swore to himself – that if he was going to have adventures in places like this, he would distance himself from the scene of the crime. He would never write news in the first-person singular.

I saw. They told me. I counted. I went. These self-aggrandising avatars, once banned in hard news, were coming into fashion. They're everywhere now. But he told himself then that he had no right to climb onstage for someone else's death scene. Nor would he complain about how those scenes made him feel. He was, at his best, a paid witness. Earn your pay honestly, and go on to the next one. If you can't accept that you're a tourist, don't get off the fucking plane.

For years, he prided himself on this old-school detachment, as if playing by the old rules could somehow indemnify him for all the adventures he would have on the back of other people's suffering, the mortgage it would pay. But maybe there was more to it than that. Or less. Maybe the *I* who he rejected wasn't general, but specific. Maybe it was specifically the *I* who couldn't bear to keep a diary, who was so dismissive about his own past, and his own achievements, that, twenty-five years later, he'd come to doubt the truth of one of the best stories he had, and certainly the best one that he could tell to his children, or to people who *weren't there*: the one about the Rain Queen. Maybe renouncing this *I* wasn't such a selfless gesture. Maybe it was just a shedding of baggage, another excuse for hurrying past.

A friend came out to live with him in Africa. The trouble with you, she said, two years later, before she finally left him, is that you fucking hate yourself. But he couldn't, or wouldn't, hear what she said. Simple answers are often wasted on young men, especially when they're unflattering. Years later, he remembered her remark, and was ready to unpack it. So he Skyped his friend Jeroen, a photographer whom he used to work with in the Middle East, and who had given up on that line of work at about the same time as he had himself. Their lives agree on several points, though Jeroen is a much better artist.

Jeroen has since gone back to live in his home town of Amsterdam, where he currently works as a bicycle courier, and gleefully self-sabotages. A late starter as a photojournalist, he spent a decade shooting the wars, won several awards, suffered a breakdown, then switched to fine-art photography and writing instead. Still, failure continues to evade him. His first collection of photographs and writings, which won international prizes, juxtaposes images of the immediate aftermath of extreme violence with moments of detached domestic beauty – tantalising glimpses of a love and a peace that are just out of reach, and might themselves be mere preludes to further outbreaks of horror, instants away.

The photography is haunting and subtle. The final short chapter, headed 'Self-Loathing', is not. In it, Jeroen writes about the night he got very drunk, alone, at home, and sent an email to the book's prospective publisher, a nice artistic man in Groningen, who had made the mistake of advising Jeroen that 'only something real' would work.

In the email, without commas or any other punctuation, I stressed over and over again how much I hated myself. How much I didn't care. I pointed out, remorselessly, how bored I was of hearing about suffering . . . When I hear other people going on about how so-and-so got killed or maimed, I just want to get the shot and go to lunch . . . The tragic thing is that much of what I wrote – drunk, maudlin, angry – is true. I realised this later, while I was sobering up. I realised that, at least in part, it has been self-loathing that has pushed me into covering conflicts. It has made me more cynical and desensitised towards others, yet it has also given me the need for an occasional pat on the back from a reader or an editor who thinks that I do what I do because somehow 'I care'. I have been like this for a long time. The wars just make it worse. They also throw in

a little extra self-pity into the mix, letting me add another notch on
my stick every time I get shot at.

Now, on the Skype call between Dublin and Amsterdam, they talk about Jeroen's latest project. Despite having no chemical training, Jeroen is working on a new technique to print black and white photographs on to fine ceramic tiles. These images will last, in principle, for thousands of years, long after our film stock disintegrates and our jpegs and RAW files age out. Listening to Jeroen, he thinks of all the old .doc files he mislaid from his computer. Fish-and-chip wrappers, mate.

Not being Irish, Jeroen is seeing a therapist. He says she has helped him to work through his stuff.

He asks Jeroen, because he's secretly hoping for a twofer, whether his self-loathing was a result of his voyeuristic, thrill-seeking line of work, or whether it might be the other way around.

Jeroen doesn't hesitate to answer. He has had this breakthrough already. It stems from having felt worthless when I was a kid, he says. I think that's why I went to Iraq, in the end. I wanted to prove myself to everyone else. I always wanted to do really good things so I would be acknowledged by other people. I'm not someone who can do simple things well and be content about it. And then one day you realise that you are taking pictures of the worst moments of people's lives and it doesn't really mean anything. And that can be hard.

Simple answers for boys. He thinks, Should I send Jeroen's shrink a residual cheque?

Jeroen seems to be happier, lately. He worries, or jokes that he worries, that his diminished self-hatred is hurting his art. Having lost touch with his various patrons in New York and Amsterdam, snubbed France's leading photographic gallery and deliberately dropped out of sight, he now works several days a week delivering food by cargo bike. He finds the work deeply satisfying. As a courier, he is considered essential personnel, exempt from any COVID restrictions. He loves the people he works with, a collection of oddballs and dropouts from all round the world.

I really want to stab myself in the eyes with a spoon when I think of the art world, he says. I've developed an allergy for the way that people talk. I need to find a new gallery to put on a big exhibition with the tiles, then I'm going to go, Surprise, motherfuckers! and just disappear again.

At the end of the First World War, the Imperial War Graves Commission asked the poet Rudyard Kipling to prepare a series of verses to remember the fallen. Published as 'Epitaphs of the War', this portmanteau poem commemorates all manner of war dead, from British servicemen to Hindu sepoys, drowned female nurses and native water carriers, heroes and cowards alike. As you'd expect from an arch imperialist like Kipling, it is racist in places, and there is a lot of finger-wagging at those who fell short of his sense of duty – for example, unionised workers in ammunition factories, or a London draft dodger killed by aerial bombing:

On land and sea I strove with anxious care
To escape conscription. It was in the air!

The shortest epitaph of all was for those who lost their lives in Kipling's original line of work, which was reporting. It consists of only five words: 'We have served our day.'

Kipling was many things, but he was also a very good poet. This short, brutal phrase seems jewel-like, multifaceted in its perfect ambivalence, its balanced regard and contempt. Is Kipling the Great Writer sneering at the toilers he left behind him, the inky grubbers who provided packaging to the fish-and-chip trade? Is he mocking the servile indignity of those who trample each other comically, like Keystone Cops, to feed the heedless, insatiable beast? Does his use of the first-person plural, as opposed to the first-person singular with which he individualises most of his other categories of war dead, target the groupthink, the hive mind to which reporters often fall victim, often because it's easier to beat the common enemy, the clock (not to mention, much more rarely, abduction or bullets), if they stop trying to beat each other?

Or is Kipling hinting at something else? The author of *Bar-*

rack Room Ballads would have known other senses of the verb 'to serve'. Soldiers in the artillery don't shoot their cannons, or operate them, they *serve* them, and are expected to keep on doing so, stoically, even as their positions are being overrun. Keep performing the repetitive, mechanical task, and hope that the big picture somehow comes good.

Is 'our day' merely a play on the *jour* in journalist, or does it point to a higher truth, which is that everything we have, or need, or love in this world is contingent on the now? There wasn't much we could do, and we don't really know why we needed to do it, but that doesn't matter, because it got done. It took Kipling only five words to say as much. Even the choice of tense, the present perfect, nods to traditional British newspaper usage. 'We have served our day', not 'we served it'. Always anchor your piece in the now or the future. Never bury your news in the past.

What was Kipling really trying to say about those dead reporters, in whom he might have recognised his younger self? Did the imperial laureate, who'd learned his trade on the North-West Frontier, reporting tribal feuds and colonial reprisals, still struggle with feelings of guilt, and pride, and disbelief, about things he had seen and done, and felt, and forgotten, when he was narcissistic and careless and young?

★

And then there's that 'we'. Instant friendships on the road, nights telling stories that could never be printed. Only nurses and cops have better yarns. You don't get sent overseas, which costs a lot of money, unless you can sing for your supper. So you didn't meet many dull people in that line of work, apart from a few of the senior Americans, rotating like clockwork through well-funded bureaus to boilerplate their résumés.

He asks Jeroen what he misses about the old days. He says, Only that. The people you worked with, the women and men from all over the world. But he himself remembers so few of them clearly. Shadows of faces. Fragments of names. You could meet someone on the road, in a hotel or bar or NGO briefing, on some out-of-the-way, off-news story, and decide to join forces, to share expenses, for the sake of an extra pair or two of eyes, and you could travel together for days or weeks, and then never see or hear from them again.

Then there were the ones he had travelled with more than once, or whom he hung around with back on base, in Johannesburg or Jerusalem, at the parties and restaurants and weekends away. There are even a few that he has stayed in touch with, people like Jeroen, because they still make him laugh, and he shares the same stories, because he *was there* too, just out of frame, when the photos were taken. But, for the most part, they lived like teens in a summer resort: everything was brighter, the days were longer, things that had happened only a short time before seemed like stones set in history; friendships felt eternal, but, when you came back a year later, or even a month, all of it was gone, no matter how sadly you looked for it. At least when a circus moves on, it moves on together. No one he knew from Jerusalem, much less from Africa, is still where he left them. Most of them went home in the end, others moved to other beats, and some of them are dead.

One close South African friend died after a long and horrible illness, having tried and failed to end it more quickly. Another – a lovely, generous woman, always scheming and cheerful, the social pivot for everyone who passed through Johannesburg – hanged herself, out of the blue.

Hansi Krauss, a wire photographer, was beaten to death by a mob in Somalia. That was before he himself first went to Africa, while he was still living and working in Dublin. Protocol demanded that someone in the trade should tell Hansi's girlfriend, a refugee who now lived in Dublin too, before the news got out. So Hansi's desk in New York rang his own desk in Dublin. And because his desk knew that he was friends with both Hansi and his girlfriend, and because he was sitting right there in the newsroom, they gave him a taxi voucher and sent him out to her house. He remembers ringing her doorbell, and nothing after that. He was twenty-six.

Myles Tierney, a producer and cameraman for APTV, was

shot dead in an ambush in Sierra Leone. Miguel Gil Moreno, another AP cameraman, died in another Sierra Leone ambush a year after that. Kate Peyton, a BBC producer, left the bureau in Johannesburg and went home to England, then decided to come back for a second go. She was shot in the back outside a hotel in Mogadishu. No machismo or adrenaline trips for gentle, slyly funny Kate: she only went to Somalia because they told her to go there, and she needed the work, and she thought that if she said no they might not renew her contract.

Word would come through, by phone or by text. You'd meet at some cafe, or somebody's house. Some people might cry, and everyone would say, Wrong place, wrong time, that's all. And then, after a while, and a couple of drinks, the refrain would change. Someone would say something like, I heard they'd met someone from Reuters earlier that morning, who'd just been out that road, and who told them that it was too dangerous. Or someone would say, I heard they had a local driver. They should have been driving the car themselves. You can't trust someone you don't know to do the right thing in a situation like that. Or someone would say, I heard they were in a hurry. They needed to file. They should have taken their time. Or someone would say, They shouldn't have gone out in the street like that, outside the perimeter.

These things were said quietly. No real blame was intended. But the myth had to be renewed, that there was always a reason why something went wrong, an error that could have been foreseen. It was important to remind the cosmos that this sort of thing shouldn't happen to *you*. But always, when the ritual was over, and invincibility restored, there would be a return to that first absolution: Wrong place, wrong time, that's all.

Of course, these deaths made the survivors' own lives seem more glamorous . . . That was something else that no one ever said aloud . . . At least he never wrote news in the first-person singular. He never broke that rule.

Except once, in his very last piece as a foreign correspondent. He went to the Gaza Strip, one last time, to write a goodbye to all that, an elegiac feature, after almost six years, and instead he came across the burning wreckage of a press jeep, minutes after its driver, twenty-three-year-old Reuters cameraman Fadel Shana, was killed by an Israeli tank shell. They were carrying off the body when he arrived. Later, when Fadel's colleagues examined what was left of his camera, they found that he had been filming the tank, a mile away, as it fired the shell that had killed him. So he had an excuse for writing in the first person: the story had already turned pretty meta.

This was the second time that Israeli forces had fired on Fadel Shana. Two years before, a drone had punched a hole through the roof of Reuters' clearly marked armoured Land

Rover. On that occasion, Fadel survived his injuries to serve another day. The wreck of that Land Rover is now the first thing you see when you enter the Imperial War Museum in London. Kipling might have preferred something more jingoistic, but it does say a lot about how war is done now.

A couple of days later, he left Gaza for the last time, walking alone across the sweep of exposed, bulldozed ground between the ruined Palestinian border post and the blast walls and towers of Israel's Erez terminal. A lone figure emerged from the Israeli side, entering Gaza. It wore a piratical black eye patch, elegant jacket and breeches, and had a fine head of blond hair. Marie Colvin. They met in the middle of no man's land, hugged, said a few quick words, and then kept going in opposite directions. This was one of the last places on earth where anyone wanted to hang about.

It was also the last time he would see her. He was done. Unlike Marie, he wasn't a lifer, or even a natural reporter. She'd been on the road for twenty-three years, and would keep going for another four, until the Syrian government murdered her in Aleppo. She had stayed there after almost everyone else left, because she hoped her reporting might bring international pressure to stop the bombardment. It wasn't the first time she'd tried to pull off something like that. She loved the adrenaline as much as anyone, and she loved to drink too much, and to join the others in reciting those bits of their favourite poems that they could remember, but she, and some others like her, also did really care.

Did it do any good? Who can say, in the long run. Marie's death didn't stop that bombardment. It's still going on. But people do like to at least have a witness. He has seen that for himself. Think of all those people with this virus, dying alone in intensive care, desperate for someone, even a stranger, to hold their hand as they go. A professional mourner is better than none. And of course, every now and then the product does come in useful. If it wasn't for that piece by Donald G. McNeil Jr, how would his kids know he wasn't lying when he told them about the Rain Queen?

May

someone who writes

he said to his wife once he said if I ever start writing about being a writer or about a fictional writer who is writing a book please get a five-pound steel lump hammer and strike me repeatedly on the back of the head

she said why wait

she didn't really say that but he could tell what she was thinking

pour the coffee go upstairs shut the box room door behind him

five thirty am maybe four hours sleep not sleeping well lately can't think very straight but try to write something now before the girls wake up and start annoying their mother she's working from home now too so use the early quiet hours to start the next chapter or essay or section whatever these things are going to be then go for a run to get your head straight it's a Wednesday so that means a short one four miles

but his phone is on the blink headphone jack no longer working and he needs music when he runs it's part of the process so what about digging out his old iPod Classic there it is in the drawer but is it still working find an old charger and test it oh good it still seems to work

but there must be a reason why he stopped using that old iPod does it jump from track to track is the battery banjaxed he can't remember he'll have to find out later he hates hearing his own footfalls when he is running it reminds him that he's running which makes it harder to not think

maybe he should fix or replace his phone maybe it's out of contract maybe he's due an upgrade look it up on the website he *is* due an upgrade but the old phone works fine apart from the headphone connection and there's too much electronic waste already and anyway these new ones are dear so why not bypass the broken headphone jack and buy some bluetooth ear buds but bluetooth ear pieces are the sure sign of a wanker or was that back in the noughties they could be OK now and surely it would be better than spending a hundred quid and several days getting the phone fixed which wouldn't be the first time and it's three years old already and he'd have no phone at all while it was being fixed and how would he get a phone fixed during this lock-down thing anyway

but he can't use regular ear buds because they fall out when he starts sweating his ears are too big but maybe they sell wireless ear buds that have those little clips that hook over the ear and let's just put the writing aside for a minute and have a look at eBay never Amazon and these ones from Scotland look OK how bad can they be only twenty-seven quid with purchase protection but they'll make him look like a wanker but so what he'll be running when he wears them so everyone will think he's a wanker anyway because runners are public enemy number one during this lockdown because walkers won't move out of the middle of the towpath when they see you coming even when you smile and nod and make eye contact and try to give them six feet they walk two and three abreast and take up the whole towpath do they expect him to swerve off into the Royal Canal do they expect him to take his chances with the swans

he told Eleven last week that he thought he could beat a swan in a fight but she thought that he couldn't he said you know it's a myth about them being able to break your leg with their wings because their bones are hollow and your bones are solid and she said they could bite you and he said birds don't have teeth and she said geese do have teeth and he said that's ridiculous and she said she saw it on a nature documentary so let's check that out now DuckDuckGo never Google oh Christ she was right except goose teeth aren't really teeth they're just cartilage so maybe he can argue they should call it a draw but then again geese are not the same thing as swans our folk tales are very firm on that point so he should stand his ground against Eleven because the fact is she's wrong about swans having teeth

sounds like someone else is up already probably Eleven now that school's out forever she likes early-morning Xbox so go down for more coffee say hi then of course start writing again

Eleven still reading in bed and it's his wife who's up early she needs an eighty-page document printed for work so she can proofread on paper but the toner warning on the printer is flashing and it's been doing that for weeks now but it still works so he'll give it a go he has a spare toner cartridge somewhere don't know where it is or how to fit it but it should be a challenge a distraction an excuse not to write it's a very basic printer have to feed the paper in by hand it will take some time to do it best get working on that now start writing again later

writers' retreats how do they work who minds the house and kids and cooks the dinners when you're off being a writer suppose it's OK if you're single but if you're single why not just work from home and if they go off for a week to finish their project which is what the writers always say they're doing when they announce on Twitter that they're going on a writers' retreat even if they get the week for free on a scholarship or a grant how can they take a week off from whatever gigs they have to do to help pay the bills maybe they have their own money or a job with paid holidays or a public-service pension but even then they'd surely get more writing done at home maybe the point of it isn't the writing they probably all get pissed up at dinner and get up to all sorts he should really read more short story collections

fucking paper keeps jamming he has to reset the printer each time and cancel the old print job start a new one from where the old one left off

beyond a joke now

Jesus

let's look it up online troubleshooting FAQs

apparently he has to take the block of printer paper and fan all the edges like a Dodge City card sharp and then he has to tap the block of paper back square and reinsert it in the printer oh wow yes that really works no more paper-feed jams but now the toner really has run out so he needs to change the old cartridge where is that spare one it's in the drawer with the iPod and Simon's old Nokia oh that was easy any idiot could do that

printing done maybe he should go for a run now try out the

old iPod and get back to work afterwards let the endorphins do their thing after the first couple of miles muscles warmed up breathing steady the music in his ear phones the ideas float out of the back of his mind without any effort his subconscious his muse don't ever call it your fucking muse is way smarter than he is just keep out of its way let the dog see the rabbit it does all the real work the fact is that he just lives over the shop

go for a run

that old iPod worked fine at least fifteen years old great idea on mile three why not write about being a writer five-pound steel lump hammer back of the head he could do it in one take Orson Welles stream of subconscious he can write really fast because he can touch-type his only true skill maybe write the whole thing on the day that it's set Dublin May 6th 2020 now there's an original idea no one thought of *that* before we could celebrate Zoom's Day by staying at home alone or with family and going no more than five Ks for our shopping and avoiding our friends and our aged parents and let the pubs all be shut so come on Dublin Tourism put a straw hat on that

but it all sounds very wanky writing about yourself it could so easily backfire if you show too much of yourself people will know what you're like and when you write about yourself you're choosing to work in your own blind spot which is pretty high risk you have no perspective like the writing they etch in a car's rear-view mirror Warning Objects May Be Stupider Than They Appear

but should definitely try writing some shorter stuff because novels aren't enough to keep you going all that rewriting and second-guessing slows you down so you only publish every five years and in between he has nothing to show for himself from one year to the next how is he going to make a living the news trade's not what it used to be no money and no hope

short stories are all very well but they kick you out just when you're getting settled like an English pub at closing time

thank God his wife has a real job though she can't go to the office because of the virus but it is driving her crazy being at home driving all of them crazy she works so hard she's so bloody diligent but at least they won't starve thanks to her though in this rip-off town you need two full-time incomes and he let her down really she didn't know when she took up with him that he wanted to write he had a proper job then though he'd just handed in his notice because he'd only just decided that he was going to try his hand at writing but he didn't tell her that for ages because he was scared of ridicule and failure and for years before that he hadn't even admitted to himself that he wanted to write though he must have known deep down because he chose English at college when everyone told him to do law or engineering or medicine or anything but arts his subconscious concealed his deviant desires but it was so bloody obvious even when he was a kid he had envied the authors of the books on the shelves in their house now *there* was a clue because envy is the lifeblood of literary endeavour but no one where he grew up ever wrote anything he's from Kildare not Wexford and he thought people would laugh at him for having notions but so what if they did and why would they care

it was like being gay but not out not even out to himself not for a long time well he's out now but he's not on the scene what a ridiculous way for an adult to live all alone in a box room making up stories but writing for newspapers was like taking methadone instead of smack it hooks on to the same neurotransmitters but doesn't give you the highs or do the lovely lasting damage he never tried smack but did most of the others which is one of the reasons why he moved back to Ireland that first time he wanted to get away from all that but also to see if he could write for himself something more than 600 or 800 or 1500 words with his heavy-handed dropped intros and his throwaway lines his outros his kickers he must have thought that he could express himself artistically via the genre of newspaper which is pretty obtuse because seriously mate it's fish-and-chip wrapping but at least he had some adventures and it paid for this house which is why he could afford to try writing in the first place because he doesn't have to pay rent or a mortgage and pity the younger ones with no

real jobs and no future and crucified by landlords and can a
true philosopher write on the rack

that French kid on Inishbofin what was his name Thibault
he asked him what he did and he said he was a writer which
was one of the first times he'd ever called himself that though
he'd been published for years he usually said he was a reporter
which covers much the same ground and Thibault asked him
what kind of novels he wrote and he said he didn't know and
Thibault was so shocked that he laughed and he said really you
don't know what kind of novels you write and it was true he
really didn't know how to say what kind of novels he wrote
though he'd published three of them already because each
one was different and he'd never bothered to come up with
an artistic manifesto but if he was French he'd have written
the manifesto first then maybe not bothered writing anything
else after because why test the truth of your abstract assertion
with a bunch of potential empirical contradictions

that's the great thing about writing it's the only branch of
the arts except maybe music where you don't have to make
up a statement before they let you start working towards
the transformation of interlocking modalities in a dissonant
matrix Jeroen had to provide an artist's statement for his
first photo exhibition so they both got drunk at Jeroen's flat
in Amsterdam and found one of these sites where you put
in your keywords and it spits out post-modernist discourse

and they were both rolling around the floor but Jeroen's gallery loved it thank God writers don't have to do that words are your business and they're meant to speak for themselves and to actually mean something and the whole point of writing is it's something you do quietly and alone like reading for that matter except now all the extroverts have taken over the business it's gotten so performative readings festivals slam poetry flash fiction writers' retreats social media what hope does a shy person have

plus you're expected to teach creative writing if you don't want to starve and he doesn't know how to do that because he never took a class he can play it by ear but he doesn't know the sheet music plus he's wary of strangers and afraid of being found out plus he doesn't want to have affairs and in the stories they write about their MFA courses everyone's sleeping with their teacher and with each other and it seems to be part of the assessment process but surely someone would want to sleep with him if he was a teacher after all he's still got all his own hair and teeth apart from that one molar he had extracted last summer and the dentist said his wisdom tooth would move to replace it except he still doesn't have his wisdom teeth which at this stage is cutting it fine

that writer he met in the pub that time the one with the master's degree in being a writer he looked kind of funny but was surrounded by women from the classes he taught maybe they want to be written about maybe that's why some women hang around a certain type of writer they hope to read about themselves being fucked in self-conscious prose but this guy's pregnant partner was in that pub too and in his book he has her face down gushing on their kitchen table and she's not the only one he writes about like that and let's hope that their kid never picks up that book and particularly not if they still have that table

he had an idea once he thought what if he wrote a story about someone who's become a published author and who wants to teach creative writing so they can make a living but they don't know how to teach because they never took any lessons because they just write from life so they sign up for a course under a false name just to learn all the shtick and the proper names for the tricks that they'd had to learn just from reading other writers but for reasons of his or her own the teacher of this course who's never really written anything starts picking on the secret author in front of the class saying that his or her assignments are shit because maybe they really are shit that would be funny or maybe the teacher is bullying the secret author to try to impress someone else in the class that the teacher fancies and whom the author fancies too that's it there's a love triangle and the author desperately wants to reveal their true identity to crush the teacher in front of the object of their mutual desire but at this point his wife would have absolutely no excuse not to be flailing away at the back of his head with that five-pound steel lump hammer

what could you tell students but to try doing two to three hours five days a week early morning is best and don't be impatient and see where that gets you and don't worry if it's shit because it always is shit at first the trick is to write it and then make it better and he wouldn't know what exercises to give the students like describe a tree or something for the love of Jesus please don't describe trees to me I know what trees look like and you don't need to be a botanist to be a writer either though from the books he's read lately you'd think that you did let the dog see the rabbit did Updike ever meet a tree that he didn't describe but look at how Tove Jansson does it she just tells you that there are mountains and that they are high and blue and your mind draws mountains that are higher and bluer than any written description just get out of the way let the dog see the rabbit or maybe just write whatever you like because this is like Hollywood no one knows anything think of all the crap that gets hyped and wins prizes and the diamonds that went through scores of rejections

he thought one time that maybe he could be a writer in residence so he applied for a few residencies until one college finally gave him an interview and the people on the panel asked him which writer friends he would bring to the festival and he said what festival and they said you have to organise a literary festival as part of the gig and he is not an organised person look at the state of his desk it's not even a desk it's an Ikea table with screw-in legs and he tried to think of all the writers he knew personally and it would have had to be a pretty short festival maybe a lunchtime event and a pizza-eating competition and the panel looked back at him politely as he sat there with his mouth open and he realised in that moment that it was back to freelance reporting for him third time lucky and he swore to himself that if he ever escaped from this excruciating interview he'd never try to be a writer again he'd be happy with being just someone who writes

an artist friend once told him that he thought writing was the purest art because you can't hide behind the form and when you're writing you always have to try to find something new and he said that for example someone had told him about a recent American novel that was only one long sentence and it had won experimental prizes and wasn't that an interesting idea and he told his artist friend that in the past five years not one but two novels that were only one long sentence had won the big English prize for experimental fiction and that Joyce first ran that experiment a century before and his artist friend laughed

maybe he could also write a story with only one long sentence in it or maybe even less than one long sentence in it or is that fewer than one long sentence maybe he could write a story with no sentences at all

Thirteen bursts into the box room she's in a panic because she's just remembered she needs a lift to the funeral of the dad of her school friend really nice guy professional chef they used to chat on the sideline at Thirteen's Gaelic football poor man just died of cancer that's the fourth one he knows this year including Charlotte

but it's only sort of a funeral because funerals are restricted because of the virus so most of the mourners will stand at the railings of Glasnevin Cemetery at least two metres apart and Thirteen will have to leave right away because there's only just time to get there before the hearse will arrive and his wife is on a work Zoom so he'll have to take Thirteen to the graveyard quick put on some shoes and a jacket it's a fresh sunny day cool wind from the east

well that was a strange one not like that one back in February the last good funeral of the year this time people lined the pavement along the cemetery railings thirty or forty of them watching in silence as the hearse drove through the gates with two cars for the family only ten mourners allowed in the mortuary chapel and no one outside said anything when the mourners got out of the cars but some waved to them through the cemetery railings and then the mourners went

into the chapel surrounded by yew trees by avenues all lined
with trees and all the rest waited out on the pavement for half
an hour though no one could hear or see the service inside
and funny thing nobody looked at their phones or talked they
all behaved as if they were inside the chapel themselves and
when the mourners came out a man in a chef's smock sang to
them through the railings The Parting Glass in a fine strong
voice though sometimes it was almost drowned by the traffic
plus the singer got choked up and he wasn't the only one

would he write it like that if he was writing this as fiction
was it too on the nose but that's what really happened the
man in the chef's smock sang The Parting Glass

life imitates art except it's better because it's true and beauty
is truth and truth beauty and all of that crack

art irritates life all that unhappiness after Charlotte died in
the spring even though he hadn't seen her for years did he
bring that on himself when he was finishing his latest book
just before she slipped away he'd been needing a legend for
two people in their twenties and he thought he'd steal from
his own past just a quick in-and-out job a smash-and-grab
raid on an old fling or two but while he was rummaging in
buried times and places he might have knocked some stuff
loose without realising that he'd done it and he forgot to bolt
the door to shut all those kids in the dark where he'd left
them and when he heard that Charlotte had gone the door

sprang open from the shock and dead years spilled out like some kind of prolapse

hilarious to think he might have brought that on himself

you have to watch what you do in there be careful mind where you step like in that novel *Roadside Picnic* the stalkers sneak into the Zone to bring out the haunted relics while corpses rise from graveyards and walk back to their old houses to return to their loved ones not zombies not scary just lonely and sad the past you can't bury and it isn't wise to turn your back on that stuff he was meant to have learned that when he was seven in his uncle Dermot's farmyard never turn your back on a skittish beast that's when you get trampled if it panics and bolts and you're standing in its way

if you give it its head you don't know what it will do to you like when he wrote that whole thing about Amundsen for his last novel his flight in an airship over the North Pole and he'd really liked the way that it read but then he took it out of the final draft fifteen thousand words of it because he didn't know what it was doing in there it didn't move the plot along and it was only years later re-reading it after that spring sent him looking back on his life for the first time in decades that he realised who he'd really been writing about that Amundsen had spent his life running from one woman to the next and one pole to the other but he was never exploring he was trying to escape himself and not looking back and that chapter had dropped from his fingertips so easily like automatic writing like falling off the bone like another fucking prolapse and he didn't bother when he wrote it to wonder why that was

he never had a manifesto and he never had a plan he just started with a feeling a glimpse of understanding and then he'd lay a trail of words towards it but he never quite got there because what did Paddy McAloon say in that song on the iPod when he was out running earlier to Prefab Sprout

he said words don't hold you broken soldiers

no the other song

he said that words are trains for moving past what really has no name

well then why bother writing at all why does anyone bother is it just so you can wave at the truth from a distance like people passing on a train like the mourners at that funeral this afternoon and why not if that's all there is it's still better than nothing but it's not all there is it's much better than that because sometimes it sings to you and when it does there is no better feeling in the world and the words spill from your fingers before your brain has time to stop them nice work subconscious and then he knows for sure that this is the good stuff there will be no second-guessing and he has to get up from the chair and walk round the box room just to bleed off some adrenaline and then he sits back down and keeps typing and he'd do nothing else for the rest of his life and he'd do it for nothing if only he could

June

Stars of Bethlehem

Eleven is now Twelve, and there will be no more school runs. She graduated from primary school in a Zoom call, two weeks after her birthday, three months after the schools shut early for the year. When she starts secondary school in September, if school starts again in September, she will walk or cycle there by herself, or perhaps with her sister, Thirteen, each alone with her phone and her music. She won't really be a child anymore, though her parents assume, they hope, that sometimes she'll still be childish.

Twelve will no longer be walked, chattering, to school by her mother. In her new school, Twelve will not be picked up at the gate by her father, as she has been for the past eight years, even after she began to get restless, and to tell him she could walk home by herself. He had resisted this change for mainly selfish reasons. For him, the school run was a chance to leave the house and see other adult faces, a window in each day. Also, he wasn't quite ready to let her childhood go.

Twelve is now almost as tall as her mother. Thirteen is taller. When they moved into this house, nine years ago, they stripped the old wallpaper in the front room and found the marks where the previous owners, a family who had been in the house for generations, had pencilled the heights of their growing children. They gathered round and looked at the lines on the wall, the faded names written beside them. Those children had stopped growing, got older and died. Now the room would be replastered, a final desecration, so, hoping to make some amends for it, the father took a photo of the marks on the wall. Then they skimmed the wall and painted it. Now that photo can't be found.

Since then, they have made marks for their own children on the frame of the dining-room door. But if they are to have any permanence in this house, after they move on, alone or together, as they will, and these marks are themselves painted over, it will be in the memories of their two children. Wherever they go, and whatever becomes of it, this house will belong to their girls for as long as they live. They will also remember the previous house, the one into which they were born, the two-bedroom artisanal in Broadstone, but mainly as a blur of light and shade, and for the year of the big snow. The house they live in now, though, will be fused to them with the heat of childhood impressions. They will remember every inch of it, and, decades later, if they live long enough, their dreams will take them back here – back home – just as their father still dreams of a house in a field in Kildare, and can see it in fine detail, asleep or awake. He can even see that house from above, from hundreds of feet in the air, because when he was younger he often dreamed that he could fly, swooping and spinning, or stepping off tall buildings, sure the air would catch him before he hit the ground.

Their father still dreams of that house, but he hasn't flown in his sleep for many years. Dreams have got small. Loose teeth. Resitting exams. Naked in public. The usual distress calls from the collective subconscious. The dream he gets most often now is so anxious, dull and realistic that it barely counts as dreaming at all. In it, he has to go somewhere in a hurry, without warning, like he often did in his old job, but he doesn't know where his passports are, or his plane ticket, or maybe his wallet, and he is frantically searching, trying to remember where he left this key to all his problems. Often, in this dream, he is trying to rejoin his family. It would be nice to be able to fly.

Does life shrink our dreams until they are mapped, on the Borgesian scale of one for one, on to our reality – coextensive, flat and dead? Is that why we never die in our dreams, no matter how vertiginous? Maybe the only dream that we can die in is our actual dream of dying, the last flicker of fading consciousness, that dream in which we actually die. But this shrinkage won't trouble the children, not for a long time, should they even be so lucky. Meanwhile, their dreams will continue to remind them of aspects of this house that their parents never understood – like, for example, how it feels to hide in the dark on the upper shelf of the airing cupboard, and what the dining-room table looks like from underneath. Beyond that, for them, still infinity.

Their house was built of red brick in the last decade of the nineteenth century and is therefore Victorian. It was part of the first privately developed terrace to go up in the village of Glasnevin, as Dublin spread out beyond her canals, swallowing farms, cottages, bona fide public houses and the country retreats of the city's elite. Jonathan Swift used to walk out here for the weekends, leaving his seat in the window at Marsh's Library, to stay with his friend, Dr Patrick Delany. Once regarded as one of the finest houses and gardens in Ireland, Delany's place was demolished in the 1950s to make way for an ugly private hospital.

The house is not particularly large, but when they moved

here from Broadstone they couldn't get over the height of the ceilings, nor the length of its back garden, where the children were meant to play football together, but seldom did, unless their father played with them. A lot of their footballs went over the walls, too many of them kicked by the father, who would trash-talk his daughters to distract them from his sad lack of ball skills. They figured this out in the end.

The house needed work and money, and got it, but it still needs a lot more. The kitchen is old and very cold, and there is talk of an extension, or a luxury shed in the garden, when and if the boat comes in. Those things would be nice. But there are other concerns too, more pressing. The double-glazed windows are ugly and plastic, and moisture has seeped into the layer of argon gas between their panes, making them look dirty even when they're clean. They could do with replacing. The rear return, which contains the kitchen, the stairs and the main bathroom, is visibly crooked, several inches off true, with a jagged crack under the stairs where it joins the main structure. When they were buying the house, their engineer did tests and took photos and measurements, and concluded that there had been flooding out back, sometime early in the life of the terrace, and that the house and its neighbours had sagged into the wet ground. You could see this in the line of the roofs at the front, he said, where the houses leaned gently together. But the engineer said that there hadn't been any movement since then, not for decades. He signed off on the structure, but advised them to fill in the crack. They still haven't filled in the crack.

What had caused that major flooding, decades ago? The River Tolka, two hundred yards to the north, has a long history of bursting its banks – its name in Old Irish means 'floody' – but the ground rises steeply between it and the back of the house, a dozen feet or more, so it can't have been that. The father suspects that the flooding might have been caused by an underground stream; he is fascinated by underground streams, working dark magic in secret. He went out the back of the house, into the unpaved lane behind the terrace, and did some mental dowsing. The lane sits in a low groove with slightly higher ground on either side of it. Old maps show that this had once been a public footpath leading down to the river, but that the grounds of the Addison Lodge hotel, recently demolished, had encroached on the old right of way, so now the lane is a dead end, narrowing as it climbs from Botanic Avenue, useful only for rear access to the houses either side. From the lie of the land, it looks as if this lane may follow the route of an old watercourse that was culverted over, like so many ancient streams in and around Dublin – the Swan River, the Nevin Stream, the Bradogue, and much of the Poddle and Camac, to mention a few. So that was one possible source of the historic flooding. There was a second, which the family discovered on a Culture Night visit to the museum in Glasnevin Cemetery. Founded in 1832 on the initiative of Daniel O'Connell, the Liberator, as a resting place for Dubliners of all religions and none, the cemetery has since gathered the remains of one and a half million people – more people than live in the city today, despite Dublin's expansion in recent years. Its eastern boundary is less than two hundred yards from their house, hidden from view by the Botanic Gardens. Yet, although invisible from this side, the cemetery is, like the Gardens, a major presence in the neighbourhood, drawing tourists and day trippers, people who lunch in the cafe at 'the Bots' and then use the side gate, recently opened, between the Gardens and the graves. Many have loved ones to visit. Some just want to walk in the peaceful cemetery – avenues all lined with trees – and read the names on the stones. Others join walking tours of the graves and monuments, or climb the 180-foot Celtic round tower that was built as a tomb for O'Connell. Admission to the museum is included when you pay for these activities, but on Culture Night, the museum is free.

One exhibit in particular caught their attention. It explained how, in the early days of the graveyard, as the number of burials increased, seepage from the corpses leached into the ground water, polluting local wells and streams, spreading disease. To fix this problem, the authorities built a network of subterranean pipes and channels, feeding a new underground river they called the Cemetery Drain. It emptied into the Tolka. The maps are vague, but they suggest that the Cemetery Drain leaves the graveyard at its south-eastern corner, passes somewhere under the entrance of the Botanic Gardens, and then either cuts through a corner of the former Addison Lodge hotel, now being redeveloped for housing, or under the end of the terrace where the family lives. Either way, to reach the Tolka it would almost certainly have to follow the course of the lane behind their house. Water can't flow uphill. Drainage never lies. For the same reason, it seems likely that, when they created the Cemetery Drain, its route must have conformed, at least in part, to the courses of existing streams and rivulets, dragging them underground with it, extinguishing their memories and names. Did one of these ancient streams flow under the lane behind the house, and does the Cemetery Drain pass under this terrace to join it? Did it once overflow, causing the subsidence that makes the terrace droop? No one knows for certain, but then no one seems to really want to. Though invisible, the cemetery is always there: when you walk among the oaks in the Botanic Gardens, the crematorium stares at you from over the wall.

By day, the graveyard can be accessed from this eastern side via its original front gate, a monumental arch, now in a quiet cul-de-sac beside the Gravediggers' pub, or by the new side gate which connects it to the Botanic Gardens. In the evening, all the cemetery gates are locked, except for one small pedestrian entrance on the western boundary, on the busy New Finglas Road. In accordance with some ancient by-law, apparently, every public cemetery has to have a gate that stays open around the clock. Or at least that's how it used to be: when the new COVID restrictions were introduced, this secret gate was chained and locked like all the others, and wrapped in the same black and yellow warning tape.

The fact that, previously, this gate was always open is not widely known, even in the neighbourhood. It was a taxi driver who told the father this, as an interesting factoid, but the father stored the information away. It came in useful eventually, though only once. Just before Christmas, a couple of years before, when his wife went up north in the car to visit her parents, he had to walk to the nearest Lidl, in the industrial estate beyond the graveyard, to pick up some food for their dinner. It was almost five o'clock, when the Gardens and the cemetery would both lock their gates, but he calculated that, if he could pass through the Botanic Gardens and into the graveyard before the linking gate shut for the night, the secret gate on the New Finglas Road would cut almost a mile off his walk, though he'd have to take the long way back. It was late December, and he thought the graveyard would be dark, like graveyards in the countryside where he'd grown up, which hadn't bothered him much. But this graveyard wasn't dark. Times have changed, and now mourners can leave LED candles on the graves of their loved ones, to remind them of home in the Christmas season. Worse, the path to the secret gate goes through the children's section, a field of fallen stars, where flickering lights showed weathered stuffed toys and freshly-wrapped presents, and the photos of children set into the stones. Try whistling past that.

It seems reasonable to assume that people have died in this house. Certainly, a lot of people have lived in it. It was built in the 1890s by Thomas Connolly, a local master builder, as part of a terrace of fourteen houses. These are listed in the 1901 census under the address of Addison Terrace – a name chosen by the developer, as was the custom of that time, and ours. The address had its roots in the early eighteenth century, when Thomas Tickell – a minor English poet, Whig activist and senior civil servant – had his country house across the road. Tickell, whose estate was later purchased by the Dublin Society to become a botanical garden, was a friend and admirer of the writer and politician Joseph Addison, co-founder of the *Spectator*. When his hero died, Tickell planted an avenue of yew trees, symbols of immortality, behind his Glasnevin house. He called it the Addison Walk, and it survives to this day as the oldest feature of the Botanic Gardens. From there, the Addison name spread into the neighbourhood. There is a housing complex called Addison Park on a bluff across the river, up Washerwoman's Hill. Addison Place is a lane off Botanic Avenue, running up behind the house, along the possible course of the Cemetery Drain. The name of Addison Lodge, the old hotel across from the Gardens, will transfer to new housing being built on its site; suburbia, the saying goes, is when you cut down the trees and name the houses after them. But Addison Terrace is gone from the map. A few years after it was built, Dublin Corporation changed the address of the houses to Botanic Road, the street that runs past them, and renumbered them accordingly. The Corporation (itself since renamed, for no good reason) didn't want to have a mishmash of addresses and numbers along what was effectively the same street; it seems there was once a time when public utility trumped private interest. But the old dispensation survives in anachronistic house numbers, now painted over, on some of the original wrought-iron gates.

The previous family had lived in this house for about ninety years. They had children and died, and their children had children of their own, and also died. And the census records show that at least two other households occupied the house before them. According to the 1901 returns for Addison Terrace, the owner was one William Albert Dawson, a thirty-two-year-old member of the Church of Ireland, whose salary as a postal sorting clerk was then enough to buy a three-bedroom house in a middle-class district two miles from his workplace in the General Post Office, the official centre of Dublin. Living with him were his wife Eileen Margaret Dawson (twenty-nine) and their sons Michael and James (three and two). Also living in the house was Ellen Norton (sixteen), an illiterate Roman Catholic general servant, or 'slavey', from County Wicklow. She would have slept in the attic, then reached by a ladder from the upstairs landing. Connolly had designed all the houses of his terrace to have a small stove at one end of the attic, connecting to the main chimney breast. Whether or not her employers gave her coal for her stove, Ellen would have slept in that corner, for the residual warmth from the fires below. It's hard not to think of her lying there still.

Ten years later, for the 1911 census, the Dawsons and Ellen are gone. The address has now been changed to Botanic Road, and the head of household is Elizabeth Lawlor, a fifty-two-year-old Dublin-born woman. She is listed as having been married for twenty years, with no children born alive, and her husband is recorded as 'not known'. Boarding with her are English-born Robert Baker (forty-four), a commission agent, John Loughran (thirty-eight) from Clare, a commercial traveller in drapery, and Dennis Delaney (twenty), a student of commercial business from County Limerick. All four are Roman Catholic.

We seem to know these people. Joyce introduced us to them: solid clerks, slaveys, middle-aged commission agents and commercial travellers, transient and precarious, and land-ladies with Mrs in front of their names but no word nor sign of the husband. Thanks to Joyce, you can still glimpse their shades on the walk – past the Brian Boru pub at the Cross Guns Bridge, along Fontenoy Street, and from Hardwicke Street corner to Findlater's Church – to Dawson's old work-place in the GPO, on which all Irish distances converge. Like us, though more faded, they are still passing through.

If anyone ever died in this house, they must have gone peace-fully. It had a welcoming feel when the family moved into it, and nothing they have done there since has managed, yet, to change that – not even in the past four months, when it became a place of semi-confinement. If some trace of young Ellen Norton still lingers in the attic, frozen in her timeline, eternally preoccupied with that transient point in her long-lost concerns, she may not have noticed these new people passing through. There have been squabbles, of course, and the par-ents are fighting a cold war for possession of the office in the box room, but on the whole they have learned to manage the cramped situation, to miss one another at point-blank range. To get out of the house, they go running or walking, and, to ease the pressure from being too close to your loved ones, they usually do it alone.

The end of June comes, and there is talk of 'opening up' and 'relaxation'. What would this mean to the mother, whose office is still closed, or the father, who seldom goes out anyway, except to go running, or to the children, whose school year petered out in March, and for whom summer is now a hypothetical concept? The girls both have their own phones now, and friends who live within walking distance – to the envy of their father, who grew up almost five miles from the nearest town – but they still haven't fully understood that their childhood is over. Their parents, frustrated at seeing them lying about the house all day, tell them they are free to go out and meet friends if they want, but still they infest the living room and rattle the door of the fridge. Maybe they've been overprotected and are frightened of the outside; maybe they are in love with the bars of their cage. Maybe they are lazy. Maybe there is too much good stuff to do at home, what with the fridge and the Xbox and all that streaming online content. Not to mention the books. Or maybe this house is too happy; when he was their age, their father would go to great lengths – almost five miles, to be exact – to stay out of the house for the day.

The girls' time will soon come, though. The signs are there already. A text-based flirtation with a kid in another school. Giggling conversations between the sisters in the kitchen, hushed when a parent comes in. Brisk walks with a Fitbit, longer and longer each day. In August, if the recovery holds good, the family will go on holiday together, to the island where they've vacationed for the past six years. But Thirteen has already announced that this year she will not go pony riding on the island, because she isn't 'some posh girl from England'. She hadn't been a posh girl from England the previous years, either; that wasn't what had changed. The parents are pretty sure that, when August comes, Thirteen will still jump off the pier with her father and her sister, and she will probably come on some of their picnics and hikes. But will she still go to Duagh beach with them on sunny afternoons, and snorkel and splash about, or will she now want to avoid them, to wander the island alone with her music, singing to herself, her head swimming with sirens and dreams? It seems pretty likely. But they'll see her at mealtimes. And they still have Twelve, just about, at least until the fall.

Even before they moved out here from Broadstone, their father would drive the girls to the Botanic Gardens several times a month, especially when it was raining. They were little more than toddlers then. The Great Palm House and the Curvilinear Range, Victorian glass palaces, offered shelter and warmth, and the chance to play hide-and-seek among plantain shrubs and Patagonian sheep-eating trees, provided there were no gardeners nearby to shush and to scold them. The Great Palm House contains an artificial rainforest, in the centre of which is a fake native hut made from straw and bamboo. Beside it, an artificial stream runs through a bed of stones and mortar, eventually disappearing through a grid into the floor, bound maybe for the Cemetery Drain. This was their favourite part of the Gardens when they were small. They would go in through the porch that contains the carnivorous plants, pausing to see if the plants had got lucky, and then they'd pass through the orchid house, push through the swinging glass door and go down the short flight of steps where Wittgenstein used to like to sit and think. (How could anyone think in this heat and humidity? Wittgenstein probably just wanted a nice sweat in a town with no saunas.) The girls would run on ahead, dropping winter coats, hats and scarves, and their father would follow them, picking up the discards, while keeping one eye on where the girls were hiding. There were only a few suitable hiding places that were accessible from the paths – inside the fake hut, under the fronds of a large shrub, or behind the overhanging leaves of a banana tree – but, left to themselves, the children might get bold and push deeper into the jungle, which was against the rules. Once, they had seen a small terrapin on a rock in the stream, presumably having been abandoned there by a bored owner, and they became convinced that this paradise contained its own wildlife. Their mother, who was with them that day, didn't tell them the terrapin was dead. Nor did their father ever draw their attention to the bait stations and rat traps under the bushes. These were clearly labelled, but the children couldn't read.

When they were a little older, the girls preferred to play outside. Towards the northern edge of the Gardens, under the little bluff above the Tolka's former floodplain, there was a small stone water feature, about three feet square, which the girls called the 'Grossness Pond'. It looked like it should have had frogspawn in it, but it never did. They would squat on their heels either side of it, poking it with sticks, fishing out the dead vegetation that collected inside it. There was also a yew tree, near the gate to the walled kitchen garden, that was good for climbing, its branches just a few feet off the ground. But climbing the trees was forbidden, so their father kept watch for them while they scrambled up the smooth, curving red trunk, looking out for the little electric buggies in which the wardens patrolled the Gardens. Their approach was silent, so you had to be alert.

One of these park wardens could be very officious, and

sometimes, when they were walking through the Gardens, they would turn and see the roof of his buggy peeping over a rise in the ground. He was tailing them from a distance, hoping to catch them breaking the rules. The father created a legend for this warden to amuse his daughters – or, rather, himself. In this reality, the warden was called Kowalski, and he was a tightly wrapped, no-nonsense parkie who liked to do things by the book, but who was prepared to bend the rules if he needed to get a result. Whenever they saw 'Kowalski' approaching in his electric buggy, their father would start humming the soul-jazz stake-out music from *The Streets of San Francisco*. The girls had never seen *The Streets of San Francisco*, or any of those old cop shows, but they seemed to get it anyway, understanding an echo from a time before their birth.

They live much closer to the Gardens now than they did then, but they visit less often, and usually alone. The children no longer climb in that yew tree, which has gotten too small as they've grown bigger, but they still seem fairly happy. Let's hope that's how they will remember this time – as happy – when they dream of this house, their forever home. We are haunted, most of all, by ourselves. Those marks on the wall don't show stages of growth but reinventions, newer versions of the child, another Russian doll to shut in all the others. Strangers still live in this house, inside the teen and the pre-teen, and inside the adults, who are trying so hard to ignore them. The big kids are in charge now, and don't want to remember their old games, but younger selves watch the world through borrowed old eyes, passing their own judgements, still dreaming former lives. New ills and lost loves, some more fretful than others, could manifest at any moment – on the crooked stairs, in the cold kitchen – and exorcise the present. They could pull a home apart. Something will, eventually. Whatever happened to the Dawsons, or Mrs Lawlor's vanished husband? But if the family can last another year or two here, there will be another census. They will have the chance to leave their own mark on that wall. And their children will always, always have been young here.

July

Tinnitus

The audiologist was a small, gently smiling woman, dressed in tasteful knitwear. Her speech, which was clear and well modulated, gave no hint of the profound hearing loss that she herself had suffered as a little girl – a genetic condition, she said.

She put him in a little booth with headphones over his ears and made him press a button every time he heard a beep. The beeps became increasingly faint as the test went on. When it was over, she told him that he had moderate to serious hearing loss in both his ears. She showed him the audiogram. Things were OK up to about three kilohertz, she said, but there was then a sudden and steep plunge in the graph, what audiologists call a 'ski slope', revealing hearing loss in the higher frequencies. Superimposed on this graph was the 'speech banana', a shaded zone containing the various meaningful sounds, or phonemes, that we use in our speech. On his audiogram, *K, F, S* and the soft, or unvoiced, *Th* of *thought* had been stranded on the wrong side of the ski slope. This meant that he could no longer hear these sounds in everyday speech, she said. He might think that he did, but, whether he knew it or not, he was lip-reading, and had been for years.

It was likely that his hearing would further deteriorate. She showed him another cluster of consonants, just to the left of the ski-slope. *P, H, G, Sh* and *Ch*. These would go next.

So *FucK*'s gone, he thought. And I'm about to lose my *Sh*it.

She recommended that he start wearing hearing aids, and she gave him a brochure to take home and study. He looked at the brochure: the cheapest of these hearing aids was still pretty dear. So he told her he'd think about it, and he did, right there and then, and what he thought, but didn't say to the lady in the test centre, was, Not yet. I'm still too young for that. I can still hear music, if I ignore the automatic safety warnings and turn the volume up full. Most of the TV and films that we stream at home have subtitles, if you want them. Besides, I can lip-read! I have a new-found skill!

He found himself strangely pleased to learn that he was going deaf. He'd always sort-of known it, but it was good to have it confirmed. He thought he understood now why he'd always been uncomfortable in large groups in bars, or at dinner; why clamour confused him, and why he'd always preferred to talk to only one or two people at a time. He thought he knew now why he'd usually withdraw into himself, or plot his escape, when he found himself in a crowded social situation, unless there was alcohol, which made it OK. He'd thought it was because he was shy of crowds, but maybe, perhaps, it was because he could only watch so many lips at one time.

His wife, on the other hand, thought it was because he was on the autism spectrum. She said it in quite a kindly way, as if she were handing him a coupon, a get-out-of-jail-free card. That would explain, she suggested, why he was often so distant, so self-involved, so absent-minded, why he said the wrong things, rubbed people up the wrong way.

But I don't do that anymore, he wanted to argue. I no longer put my foot in it with people. I've grown. Then again, he realised, he didn't meet new people very often anymore, not since the kids had arrived. Could she be right? And how would he know if she was?

He tested his wife's belief on his old friend, Seán, whom he met in Toner's one afternoon towards the end of July. It was the first time either of them had been in a bar in five months, and would be the last time for who knew how many more.

The place was empty, at first. They each had to pay nine euros for a ham and cheese sandwich before they could order the first of too many drinks.

Seán told him that of course he was autistic, or a bit Asperger's, or something. Everyone said that about him, including all their friends. Seán said all this with a contented smile, as if he too was offering a blessing.

He told Seán that he didn't agree; he was just a bit deaf. It seemed to him that autism had become fashionable lately, that some people staked a claim to a place on the spectrum in the same way that they might otherwise discuss their fascinating allergies and food intolerances, whether or not these were real. Some even boasted of being 'high-functioning', as if this were proof of their own supremely cool and sharp focus – these were the kind of people who might otherwise claim to be spiritual, or to have an artistic temperament. It was cultural appropriation, he told Seán. Real autism wasn't a joking matter. Besides, the preferred term now was 'neurodiverse'.

Seán said he could speak with some authority on the matter because he was on the spectrum himself. It was something he thought they had in common: why else had they been friends for so long? When he was younger, Seán had serious issues with obsessive compulsion, washing his hands until they were swollen and sore. Seán had tunnel vision; once he started something, he had to finish it, no matter how pointless it turned out to be. There was other stuff too, Seán hinted vaguely. Besides, Seán and his wife had genuine knowledge of the subject: they had a teenage son who really was profoundly autistic, and profoundly deaf.

Listening to Seán, he began to wonder for the first time if maybe his own people were right about him. Am I deaf, he wondered, or is there more to it than that? And of course, both things could be true at once. Perhaps he should also get tested for autism spectrum syndrome, while he was at it. It was too late to do much about it, at this stage of his life, but he could use the excuse, if not the diagnosis. Turns out, it wasn't my fault that I've always been an awkward bastard: it's just how I'm wired. But he didn't think he deserved any such absolution. The signs just weren't there. He didn't stim, for instance – though, when he thought about it, he some-times had a restless leg, and a stutter. Were those symptoms of something, other than nerves? He didn't know. He should look it up. Sometimes, rarely, when he was very frustrated, or felt himself put upon to an unusual degree, he would smack himself on the side of the head, as if one of the Three Stooges had been left alone and had to fly solo. But that wasn't so odd, was it? He didn't do it so hard that it would hurt, much. He'd barely noticed himself doing it – although the last time he had done it, he'd noticed his older daughter, who was in the room at the time, noticing him doing it . . . OK, he *was* uncomfortable talking to strangers, and also most of the people he knew, but everyone knows that people are hell. He also had severe difficulty in admitting new people into his world, in remembering their faces and names, even moments after he'd met them – a crippling affliction in his old trade as a reporter. But lots of people were like that, right? And – he told Seán, as they ordered their third round – he'd read that autistic people feel uncomfortable looking other people in the eye, that this was one of the surest signs of the condition, even in high-functioning people, and he didn't have that problem. Surely that was a clincher. He was in the clear . . . Although maybe, now that he thought about it, it wasn't their eyes he'd been looking at. Maybe he'd been reading their lips.

The problem, whatever it was, had gotten worse lately. He'd gone to Boots the day before, to renew his asthma prescription, and the young woman behind the counter had to repeat herself three times before he understood what she was saying – Should she hold on to the prescription, for the next time he came in to fill it? At first, he thought she was foreign, but, after he put his ear right up to the plastic shield in front of the till, he realised that she had a normal Dublin accent. It was her mask that had tricked him: he couldn't see her lips when she spoke. Instead, he'd had to look into her eyes. Which, he realised, made him feel uncomfortable.

He decided that next time he got some spare money, which

wouldn't be any time soon, with the gig economy the way it was, he would go back to that audiologist and talk to her about hearing aids. If he had to cop to something, he'd stick with being deaf. He already had that one in the bag.

The audiologist said that a steep dip in sensitivity between three and four kilohertz was a strong indicator of noise-induced hearing loss. Had he been exposed to very loud noises at some early point in his life?

He thought about that. His hearing had been poor since he was in his teens, if not before. He remembered the tractor, when he was fourteen. Driving twelve hours a day, six or seven days a week, all summer long, turning mown grass with a hay bob, to dry it out before baling it for hay. The tractor was an International Harvester, too small, at that stage in tractor evolution, for luxuries like sprung suspension, a noise-proof cab, or power steering. To operate the hay bob, you had to steer the tractor in ever-decreasing rectangles, conforming with the shape of the field, starting at the headlands, under the hedges, and working your way into the centre. You were battered by the sound and vibrations of the big diesel engine, shaken by the jolting of the unsprung wheels, worn out by the heavy unassisted steering, by wrestling with the harsh right-angle turns, coming quicker and quicker as you neared the middle of the field and the rectangles got ever smaller. The hay bob – two whirling horizontal wheels set with protruding steel prongs – picked up the mowed grass and tossed it in the air, fluffing it up like a pillow, spreading it out to dry in the wake of the tractor. When you finished turning one meadow, you went and turned another, then another, then back to the first one and turned it again. Their farm had been financed with loans in a fat time, just before a big slump, and now they were trying to get out from under this debt by selling large amounts of hay to the local horse industry, renting conacre from other, less intensive farmers to make high-grade feed for the stables on the Curragh. This hay had to be good; the half-green, weedy crap that some farmers fed to their cattle wouldn't do for thoroughbreds. Worse, if you packed bales of wet, green hay tight in a barn, it could start to ferment, and overheat, and spontaneously catch fire. So after you mowed the long grass, you turned it and turned it and turned it, spreading and re-spreading it until its colour changed from green to yellow-grey, and then you reset the teeth on the hay bob and narrowed the gates that protruded behind it, so that, with your final pass, the hay would be piled in a neat fluffy ridge, ready for the baler. And then, as likely as not, it would start to rain, and, when it stopped, you had to reset the hay bob and begin spreading the hay out to dry it again. When he'd finished in the evenings, after ten to twelve hours of this, he felt bruised and jelly-legged, as if he'd been playing football all day. He still heard the engine drumming late into the night.

It was, he decided now, almost forty years later, one of the best jobs he'd ever had. He'd been trusted, still a boy, with valuable equipment and a grown man's job – driving. Best of all, he'd worked alone, lost all day in the geometry, in the right-angle turns, and in the tunnel of concentration that transformed the unturned hay in front of the tractor into fluffed-up hay behind it. Hours vanished in this gaze. Mirages floated in the dust and fine chaff thrown up behind the tractor, shimmered along the blurred and mysterious frontier between the hay he'd just turned and the hay he was now turning – micro geographies, phantom islands, mirrors of the inner mind, like the landscapes of Gerard Murnane.

Things didn't work out, at home or on the farm, which had to be sold. A couple of years later, like a lot of the boys in his home town, he joined the part-time army reserve. This had been a garrison town since the time of the British, and many of the other boys were hoping to follow fathers or brothers into the regular army – prior reserve service was a plus with the recruiters. Others, like him, joined because you were paid good money for guard duties in the barracks, and for summer training in the Glen of Imaal, which was also very beautiful.

You were meant to be seventeen when you joined, as with the regular army, but there were ways around that. In neutral Ireland, there was little chance that you'd ever hear, or fire, a shot in anger. You could leave any time you liked, so the regular NCOs couldn't be too hard on you. Plus, although you were only playing at soldiers, you got to do it with real weapons, which was fun for a kid who'd grown up watching war films with his dad.

The local reserve unit happened to be a field artillery regiment. As a gun-layer – the member of the crew who actually aims the piece – he had to be able to hear the angles of bearing and elevation called out by the command post, so he could set them in his sights. In practice, this meant that he and the other layers couldn't wear their issued ear defenders. But he didn't think it was this that had damaged his ears. Their regular instructors had taught them an old gunners' trick for protecting their hearing: when you know you're about to get the order to fire, cup your hands over your ears, stare at the breech block, open your mouth and scream. It opens the tubes up, equalises pressure, lessens the shock. And this had worked pretty well.

But you couldn't hold your hands over your ears when you were firing a rifle, or other small arms. Plus, screaming would have been frowned upon in such a context. Once, he had briefly made it on to the battery rifle team, despite being only an average shot. One Sunday, the battery spent the morning on the ranges on the Curragh, qualifying on light machine guns, and then the rifle team stayed behind for the afternoon to practise for a competition. They'd each fired hundreds of rounds that day, with no ear protection. That night, he could barely hear his family speak for the ringing in his head. It was like that for weeks, maybe longer, then it gradually faded. But had it ever gone away, or had he just learned to forget to hear it?

That same day, when he came home from the double session on the range, his ears singing to him like jet turbines, he had found three live rounds of rifle ammunition in the pocket of his combat jacket. He had failed to use up all his rounds in one of the timed practices, the falling plates, having run out of time because of a jam, and he had stuffed the spares in his pocket, then forgot to turn them in afterwards. He hadn't done this deliberately: he was pretending to be a good pretend soldier, and besides, the possession of live ammunition was a serious offence.

What should he do with these buckshee bullets? Hand them back in? If he did that, he might get in trouble with the range officer, who'd be embarrassed for not having noticed them gone. In the end, he said nothing, and put them in the Jacob's biscuit tin where he kept his boyhood treasures – photographs, curiosities, badges for bands that he liked, letters from pen pals, and from the American girl whom he'd kissed on a school trip to Paris. Things like that. This box was stored on the upper shelf of the wardrobe in his bedroom. He opened it less and less often as the years went on, after he went off to college in Dublin, finished college, started working. Eventually, while he was living in Africa, the house went up for sale. Most of its contents went into storage, including the box. At some point, several years later, after his brother Simon had died, the storage bill stopped being paid. The explanations for this were vague, apologetic. But at some point, all the stuff in storage had just gone away.

He didn't complain. He understood what had happened. It was better that way. In their house, after their grandfather died, when appliances broke they didn't repair them, or at least, not for a long time. Nor did they throw them away. They left them there, as silent reproaches, until the need to repair them was urgent, or a new one was bought. In this case, the stuff in the storage unit, wherever it was, would only have brought back old sorrows. But so – even more so – would deliberately throwing it away. Better to let it slip into the silence. As for those three bullets, they were harmless, unless you loaded them into a gun.

That's what he had told himself, the first time he pulled those three shiny brass rounds from his pocket. There would be no harm in keeping them, squirrelled away. But it didn't work that way. Those illicit rounds turned out to be seeds. They germinated in the dark of the closet, and grew, and turned into a loaded rifle. He developed a recurring dream in which he had stolen an actual weapon and ammo from training, smuggled them home, and had hidden them in the back of his wardrobe, just for fun. Or just in case. That phantom rifle, an FN automatic, was like a telltale from Poe. What was he going to do with it, anyway? What would happen when the army missed it, and started to look for it? They were bound to find it, and then he'd be in serious trouble. Ireland has little tolerance for unlicensed hunting guns, much less for stolen military weapons. He'd go to jail. His life would be ruined. The rifle was there in his closet, or sometimes hidden under the floor, waiting to destroy him. He should throw it in a river, or bury it in a ditch. Sometimes he was about to do that, and then he'd wake up.

Those bullets are long-gone, but the dream still recurs. He'd never bothered to read deeply into psychology, or the interpretation of dreams, and he'd never even thought about seeing a therapist; he had considered himself to be more happy than he had any right to be. Also, it was his horror of confession, more than anything, that had turned him away from the Catholic Church, just as soon as he'd banked his confirmation money. In any case, he had learned to live with his collection of recurring dreams. They didn't even count as nightmares, really. More like annoying old friends. Plus, they were wasting their time. They didn't tell him anything he didn't know when he was awake. He didn't need a dream to remind him that, like many of his nation, he was excessively fond of guilt. And he knew perfectly well why someone like him might dream of owning a secret gun, and yet also be repelled by it.

Had the ringing in his ears gone away, in his younger days, for a while at least, or had he just learned not to hear it, until recently? Certainly, the sound had changed with time. Now, it wasn't a ringing so much as a hiss, backed up by a whistle, a bit like the sound the old analogue TVs made when they showed you a screen full of snow. Did its signal fluctuate, growing louder and softer during the day, or was it his attention to it that waxed and waned? Sometimes, when it was in a friendly mood, it sounded like an old leaky tap.

One night he was lying in bed, trying to sleep, when he suddenly became hyper aware of the sound in his ears. It seemed louder than ever, and it was ringing again, as if he'd just come off that firing range, thirty years before. This jolted him fully awake. It was as if some familiar, harmless animal – a pet, or a farm beast, something tame and unremarkable – had sneaked up behind him, and he'd only turned and noticed just before it could attack. It wasn't that he hadn't known it was there, but it usually did its own thing in the background, politely ignoring him. But now here it was, louder than ever, demanding attention. What does it want from me? he wondered. He knew that it wouldn't go away, that it would always be there, but what if it forgot the restraint it had shown until now? What if it wanted to destroy him? What if it decided to drive him insane?

He picked up his phone, turned the screen to night mode, so as not to wake his wife, and looked it up online. He was right to be worried. Some people were driven mad by their tinnitus. Some were driven to kill themselves. They had a demon lodged in their skull, and they couldn't exorcise it, so they took it down with them. He thought, Could that happen to me? What if it turned against him, a toothache in his mind, and made ordinary life – thought, work, sleep, human contact – impossible? What if it defined him? What if it became all that he had?

This thought terrified him. He lay there for a long time – or at least, for many long seconds – unable or unwilling to breathe. Deprived of the shield of the sound of his breathing, he had to face the tinnitus on its own terms. It sat on his chest, a hissing succubus, a one-note siren, daring him to try to escape. But he knew that if he did, it would chase him down and destroy him. There was only one other thing to be done.

He forced a deep, ragged breath. He would have to *make friends with it*. After all, he told himself, things could always be worse. The day that it left him would be the end of everything. So he coined himself a mantra, one he often repeated thereafter when something drew his attention to the singing in his ears: With tinnitus, you are never alone.

And he thought, that first night, having made this resolution, Is this what growing up means? Have I just managed to be *wise*?

Now there was a third player in this game. On another night, a couple of years after he had befriended his tinnitus, he was lying in bed again. This time, his wife was awake. They were both reading. And he had turned to his wife, cross, and wondered aloud, How long are those roadworks going to continue? And why do they only do them at night?

She had put down her book and looked at him over her glasses.

What roadworks?

Those roadworks out the back of the house, a few hundred yards away. Or, if it wasn't roadworks, that construction, off in the middle distance. He'd been hearing the humming of the diesel compressor for what seemed like months, now, but when he went out by day he never saw any sign of such work in the neighbourhood.

His wife stared back at him, as if she thought he might be joking. There was no sound of construction behind the house. No compressor or generator. No buzzing sound, apart from the noise of distant traffic, which was thin at this time of night. He must be imagining it.

He listened again, that night, and for many nights after. I'm not imagining it, he thought, I'm hearing it. Although that didn't necessarily mean it was real. He consulted his phone again, typing 'mysterious buzzing sound' into a search engine. And that was how he first learned about the Hum.

The Hum is a mysterious low-frequency noise which is heard by millions of people all over the world. It is typically compared to the drone of a diesel generator, somewhere in the distance. In some places – like Taos, in New Mexico, or Windsor, Ontario – the Hum is more intensely localised, and a higher proportion of people say they can hear it. In other places, only a tiny percentage of people claim to be sensitive.

The most likely explanation for the Hum is that it is another form of tinnitus, feedback in the interface between the mechanics of the ear and the nerves of the brain. Yet this explanation isn't entirely satisfactory. Many people who hear the Hum, he read on his phone, only hear it at night, or in one room of their house, or say that it disappears when they move to a different place. Some scientists claim to have succeeded in recording it, isolating it from all the other noise in the environment, from wind, traffic, waves on distant shores, the radio static that comes from the stars, and from the Electronic Voice Phenomenon, the ghosts that are said to manifest in recording equipment. In some places, like Windsor, Ontario, the Hum has been positively linked to nearby industrial sites or transformer stations; when these are then shut down, the Hum disappears. In other places, intensive acoustic surveys have conclusively identified the local source of the Hum, typically in some nearby factory or generator, but the Hum hasn't stopped when it is switched off. Some scientists – and he wondered how closely he should examine their credentials, because he was enjoying this rabbit hole, late at night, with the phone screen turned to night mode – have theorised that the Hum is the sound of the planet itself, its resonant tone, which is why only a few people, whose skulls or inner ears resonate at the same frequency, can hear it. Only they can hear the earth singing as it sails through time and space. It is a softer, lonelier sound than the whine of tinnitus.

The Wikipedia page for the Hum had links to related articles about mysterious sounds. He learned from these about the fifty-two-hertz whale, whose calls have been recorded, for more than thirty years, roaming the North Pacific. The experts think it might be a blue whale, or a fin whale, or even a hybrid of the two, but, for reasons unknown, it sings at a much higher frequency – at fifty-two hertz – than the other large whales that share its patch of ocean. Which means that the other whales either can't hear it, or don't recognise its calls as coming from one of their own. It's on a different spectrum. Scientists have been trying for years to get a look at this whale, but no one ever has. Some think it might be injured, or a freak, but the longevity of its wandering, plus a gradual deepening in its voice, suggest ageing and growth, which means it must be living and feeding successfully. There is a theory that it is a normal whale who was born profoundly deaf, and never learned to sing in tune with its own kind.

He had never heard of the fifty-two-hertz whale before that night, but he learned now that it was already a media darling. Someone had given it a romantic name: the Loneliest Whale in the World. Documentaries had been made about it, and animated films. Songs and books and articles were written. A lonely, hopeful soul, swimming alone in a vast, cold sea, calling to ghosts who will never reply. It writes itself, really.

The existence of the Loneliest Whale in the World was first discovered by the US defence establishment. During the Cold War, the US created networks of underwater microphones and magnetic sensors to monitor the movements of Soviet submarines. This game of cat and mouse outlived the end of the Cold War, and the abyssal plain still has its secret ears, puzzling over strange noises. The submarines themselves, like whales, sometimes use eerie, ultra-low-frequency sound for submerged communications. Other strange, recurring undersea noises, with names like 'upsweep', or 'whistle', or 'bio-duck', are thought to be caused by ice shelves grinding on the sea floor, or by avalanches on the continental shelves, or by shrimp clicking their claws, or the mating calls of toadfish, or the songs of as yet undiscovered species of whale. Some, like the Hum, still have no fully accepted scientific explanation. He hoped they never would. And, while he wished it well with its search for friendship, he hoped no one ever set eyes on the Loneliest Whale.

In his last novel, he had written about the Distant Early Warning Line, a network of Cold War radar stations from Greenland to Alaska. In his imagination, these radar stations – isolated in the high Arctic, reached only by air, staffed by small crews of air force and civilian technicians – were the cells of latter-day ascetics, like the early Irish monks of Skellig Michael, who clung to their rock in the storm-blown Atlantic to face down the devils that live in our loneliness. In his conceit, these DEW Line stations peered not only towards Russia, watching for nuclear bombers coming over the pole, but above and beyond that, on a tangent to the planet, past the point where lines of longitude converge and – in another life or dimension – separate again, reaching into the forever.

For him, the DEW Line technicians were initiates in a secret quest. He suspected he wasn't alone in this notion. When the US and Canadian governments revamped the radar network, and renamed it the North Warning System, most people in the high north stuck to the old name: Distant Early Warning. Any fool could tell it was much more poetic.

He'd grown up during the Cold War, and, like many of his generation, he sort of missed it now. The possibility – probability, it had seemed – that he and everyone he knew would be annihilated at short notice by thermonuclear weapons, whether by accident or on purpose, was terrifying, but at least it would have been tragic. The present reality, of a slow, onanistic auto-asphyxiation, in which only the 0.01 per cent will achieve sterile orgasm before the planet chokes out, seems farcical at best. Not even a bang for our bucks. And if we had pushed the button, back in the good old days, most life on the planet would probably have survived us. The Chernobyl exclusion zone, now teeming with nature, has shown us that. Now, it could already be too late.

Because of this Cold War nostalgia, he did a lot more research on the Distant Early Warning Line than ever made it into his book. It was this that had led him to nuclear submarine warfare and the US Navy's undersea Sound Surveillance System, the network of submerged listening devices designed to track submarine movements, which had first recorded the fifty-two-hertz whale. Nuclear bombers may no longer fly permanent patrols over Lancaster Sound and Ellesmere Island, praying to receive the periodic go/no-go failsafe signals, relayed from the DEW Line, ordering them *not* to attack, but the nuclear submarines are still out there, playing tag in the abyss. He had become fascinated by what little he could learn about this secret war, one in which a shot has never been fired, but that is still fought for real, every day of the year. The large, quiet ballistic-missile submarines still slip from their bases at Holy Loch in Scotland, or Russia's Kola Peninsula, often hiding under other vessels or submarines to obscure their escape, and make their way, stealthy and slow, to attack positions from which, if the right codes are sent, they will launch salvoes of thermonuclear missiles, each capable of destroying a whole city and its hinterland. The hunter-killer subs, smaller and faster, still go out and try to shadow the enemy missile boats, ready to fire their own torpedoes the moment war is declared or the order comes through.

As a boy, the thought of auto-genocide had naturally repelled him. But now, having matured, he saw some beauty in its details. He imagined these submariners as undertakers for a fallen humanity. If they ever performed their secret ministry, if the last signal they ever received wasn't a drill, then they could be the last survivors of our species. Their boats could stay down deep practically forever, thanks to the power they draw from their nuclear reactors. Their human crews could endure for months before they ran out of food, or went mad.

As he got older, and the nights grew more anxious, he learned to soothe himself to sleep by imagining himself as a submariner, snug in a round black hull, preserved by steel plates, only a few inches thick, from the enormous dark pressure outside. He would glide far beneath the seasick surface, warmed by the endless power of the nuclear reactor, engrossed in some technical task, cradled in the greater silence. The camaraderie was said to be warm and strong, with no place down there, where everything was contingent on close cooperation, for the bullying and hazing of surface life. The food on submarines, atypically for military service, is said to be good. And this would be a musical war. Once submerged, the submarines could only detect each other by what little sound they made with their engines, reactors and air-conditioning equipment, or by clumsy sailors dropping, say, a five-pound steel lump hammer on a steel deck. The sonar operators sat in their soundproof compartments and listened to the world in their headphones. They learned to distinguish the snapping of shrimp, the singing of whales, the crackle and pop of shifting polar ice floes, and the faint whisper that could be the muffled screw of an enemy submarine, perhaps in the distance, perhaps only yards away. Were you stalking it, or was it stalking you? All of it, out there, in the cold and the blackness, for your blind amazement, and yet here you were, in the warmth and dim light, waiting for mealtime and the next change of watch.

He knew that when he summoned this dream to help himself fall asleep he was self-soothing, as Simon had done with his fantasies of the Yukon, of living snug and alone in the polar night. They were both, like Proust's ageing Aunt Leonie, weaving their own cocoons: having been outside and had a good look around, they were shopping for new wombs. He knew that his submarine dream was an infantile fantasy. For one thing, with his hearing, he would never have been given a job that required listening to anything.

Nor did he think he'd have lasted very long in the con- fined space of a submarine. A few years before, when the girls were still toddlers, he'd taken them for their first visit to the five-thousand-year-old passage grave at Newgrange; as their tour group waited outside, he had looked at the narrow, low entrance, roughly three feet square, and felt a squirming in his stomach as sweat trickled in his hair. His children had sneaked to the front of the queue and were calling him to join them, but he couldn't move. And the young tour guide had noticed his face, and had raised his voice, as if he were talking to the group in general, and said that if anyone felt a little uncomfortable about tight spaces, they should hang back and go in last, so they'd be able to see that the passage behind them was clear, in case they felt any sudden desire to leave in a hurry. That way, they wouldn't panic, the kindly tour guide had said. So that's what he'd done, and it had worked, just about. He'd saved face with his daughters. But the experience left him shaken. He'd been inside Newgrange before, several times, when he was younger – once, even, in the pre-dawn blackness of the winter solstice itself, when, had that morning been clear, which it wasn't, the first rays of the sun would have shone down the ancient passage and lit up its womb – and he didn't remember any previous uneasiness. Was late-onset claustrophobia also a thing? What else lay in ambush on the road ahead?

And why, if he was claustrophobic now, did he still like flying so much, even though planes were also constricted? Was it because you could always look out? That spring and that summer, as the world closed in by day and the walls loomed at night, submarines faded from his pre-sleep routine. They were replaced by an alternative surrogate womb, one he'd discovered down a similar rabbit hole. He'd researched, for his last novel, how the vast Canadian Arctic was mapped, in a hurry, by a few squadrons of under-resourced airmen, just after the Second World War, and it led him to the history of 413 Squadron, Royal Canadian Air Force. During the war, this squadron had been based for a time at Castle Archdale, in Northern Ireland, attached to Coastal Command, flying long-range patrols of the Western Approaches. Their Canso flying boats operated low and slow, under the weather, searching for a glimpse of a submarine's conning tower in the trough of a swell, or for the feather of spray thrown up by a periscope, or – in the shadow campaign of the North Atlantic weather war – for German spy ships sneaking meteorologists into the fjords of eastern Greenland.

He imagined young men, staggering under their heavy wool and leather flying kit, loaded into dinghies and rowed out, in the cold small hours of Fermanagh winter nights, to the waiting outlines of their aircraft, riding at moorings in the black of Lough Erne. He heard the engines fire up, saw moorings slip, a plane rising on to the step of its hull, skimming the lough, breaking free of the water; a low, climbing turn, to haul its full load of fuel and depth charges clear of Cuilcagh Mountain. The sun would rise behind it as it flew across the Donegal Corridor, the narrow strip of neutral Irish territory which was, by secret agreement, violated every day by patrolling Allied aircraft. And then it would be over the cold North Atlantic, en route to its assigned patrol box, where it would fly for a day and a night in geometric patterns, all eyes on the sea.

He had read somewhere, online, that it was possible for a Coastal Command crew to complete a whole tour of duty without ever seeing any sign of the enemy. And yet they had done their job just by flying around: they might not have seen their enemies, the U-boats, but the submariners would have seen and heard them in the distance, and been forced to dive for concealment, switching off their diesel engines, draining their short-lived batteries, reducing their speed to the much slower rate of their electric motors, so they could no longer keep up with the Allied surface convoys. He had seen for himself that war was ordinary life, accelerated. This seemed like a peaceful way to go to war.

He imagined himself as a gunner-observer, sitting alone in one of the round glass bubbles set in the sides of the flying boat. These Cansos – or PBYs, or Catalinas, whatever you wanted to call them – were very slow, but they could stay in the air for twenty-four hours. How would that feel, to sit in a glass bowl for a day and a night, staring down on a cold and vacant ocean? What would you see there, and what would you hear? These aircraft were unpressurised and unheated, their engine noise unshielded. Crewmen were expected to stay off the intercom unless they had something to report; only the odd snatch of talk in his ears, between pilot and navigator, would tie him to the rest of humanity. He imagined the geometric patterns of the search, the sea brushed into lines by the sun and the moon and the wind, the hypnotic crawl of the deep ocean swell, clouds piled on horizons like undiscovered lands. He saw the stars rising and setting under the wing, and heard again the drone of heavy engines, visions dancing in his head. And he imagined the homecoming, the plane back at its moorings, a waiting rowboat, legs like jelly, body exhausted by the buffeting of the aircraft, dazed eyes, and the insistent sound of motors, now shut down, still ringing in his head. He thought he might have been able for such a job.

August

In Another Life

Twelve had discovered a new favourite song, and she played it over the car's speakers whenever they went swimming. Summer was ending, so they went to the beach as often as they could, while the good weather lasted. The song she had found was an old one: 'Once in a Lifetime', by Talking Heads. He had first heard it when he was only a year or so older than Twelve was now, although then it was new.

This song had always seemed to him to refer to the line from *Julius Caesar*, that there is a tide in the affairs of men that, taken at the full, will lead to fortune – in the song, to a large automobile, and a beautiful house, and a beautiful wife – but that, if you miss it, will leave you trapped in the shallows for the rest of your life. Except that the songwriter,

David Byrne, takes Shakespeare's notion one stage further, to the point where that tide, seized and exploited, has turned again, and you realise you are far out to sea, and the shore is out of sight, somewhere far behind you. In the back seat, Twelve sings along happily with this second-hand epiphany: *And you may ask yourself, Well, how did I get here?* . . .

Her father was beginning to worry that Twelve's choice in music was a little too on the nose. Who was writing this story? Or maybe she was on the same voyage that he was, except several tides behind. He hoped not, for her sake. One writer in the family was already one too many, as far as the ration strength went.

Sarah, a friend from the old days, called him that August to tell him that a mutual friend, Tommy, had died. They used to hang around together, for a while, three decades before. She wanted him to know that there would be a funeral. It was meant to be private, she said, but, if he wanted to come, there would probably be room in the chapel. Social-distancing rules had been eased, at that point, and it would be a small funeral. Although he'd grown up in Dublin, Tommy had spent his latter years living alone down the country. Not many people would travel that far for the funeral, the way things were.

He wondered, is it really my place to go? He'd liked

Tommy well enough, when he'd known him, but it was Sarah who'd brought them together. She was what they'd really had in common. On the other hand, she sounded sad on the phone. And he was grateful that she'd included him, all these years later. He wouldn't have heard about Tommy's death otherwise. He wasn't old enough, yet, to check the deaths every day.

Tommy would be buried in the cemetery out by the airport, under the flight path of final approach. As it happened, Tommy had always loved aeroplanes, and had worked in aviation for a while. Now, his mourners had to wait outside the chapel for the previous funeral to have its allotted few minutes, and, standing in a wide circle with Sarah and several faces from their old days, he noticed that only one plane came over in almost ten minutes – this, on the threshold of what would normally be one of Europe's busiest runways. He thought of the missing man formation, and of how it always seems to rain on television funerals. Tommy was getting his own kind of send-off.

When the previous funeral cleared out of the chapel and the new people filed in to replace them, Tommy's music was already playing: This Mortal Coil's cover of 'Song to the Siren', an anthem from their time. Afterwards, outside, he asked Sarah about the choice of music. She said she would have picked a Microdisney song, 'Everybody is Dead', but she didn't have a download. It had been Tommy's favourite song, she said. Which made sense: it was, like Tommy, both funny and sad. Still, he was surprised to hear that Tommy had loved this particular song, which was also his own favourite track by Microdisney; he hadn't even known that Tommy liked that band. Turned out, they *had* had something else in common, apart from Sarah. He told Sarah, now, that 'Everybody is Dead' was in the music library on the phone in his pocket, that he had burned that whole album from an old CD. They could have plugged it into the speakers and played it for Tommy. Sarah shrugged and made a crooked smile. Next time, she said.

When he was nineteen years old, working for the summer on building sites in London, he had taken LSD with some friends from his home town. It was the first and only time he ever did acid, and, as was his habit with most things, he had taken too much. Sometime in the early hours, before the euphoria segued into hours of horror, the drug showed him a vision from another life.

His family had left Canada in a hurry, in circumstances that he never fully understood, when he was about five years old. Their mother's mother, the Fermanagh-born matron of St Joseph's hospital in Whalley Range, Manchester, was dying, and their mother, an only child, had to get back to see her before it was too late. There must have been other stuff too, something to do with their parents' marriage, because they never went back to Edmonton after their grandmother died. Instead, they stayed with their grandfather in Manchester, without their father, for another year, before rejoining him in his native Kildare, where the family would settle. Now, sitting in a flat in Finsbury Park, the drug showed him a glimpse of himself, and his brothers and sister, as they might have been if they'd stayed in Manchester and grown up there instead. They would have been English, pretty much, like their mother. Their mother would probably have been happier in her home town. Our Lady's primary, just around the corner from their grandfather's house on Carlton Road, in Manchester, had seemed a bit rough after their Edmonton Montessori, but it was a playschool compared to what awaited them in Catholic Ireland. Had they stayed in Manchester, the acid hissed at him, they would have lived more open, orderly lives, amid the mature trees and dead leaves and dripping red brick that he recalled of Whalley Range. He saw himself wearing slacks and a woollen V-neck jumper. His alternative self was boring but contented. He wasn't the type who would have gone off the rails a bit, or been in trouble at school, or ever taken acid, even the once.

All happy families are alike, Tolstoy wrote, but each unhappy family is unhappy in its own way. He'd always liked the sound of this, but he didn't think that it was true. The LSD clearly agreed with Tolstoy, in so far as it equated contentment with boredom, but it had seemed to him, as he grew older, and learned the truth about other families around his, ones that he'd envied and admired for their apparent warmth and tranquillity, that happy families were so rare as to each be unique. Unhappy families, on the other hand, were much of a kind. There were only a few basic ingredients, and you didn't need all of them, or very much of each. You needed, for instance, someone who drank, back then, in secret. People who had got married much too young, the first chance they got, presumably *because* they were so young and, in that time and place, you had to get married before you could live together. People who, it soon turned out, even on their best days, weren't suited at all, but felt they had to make a go of it, because they'd had kids before they were ready. You didn't need to experience violence, or adultery, or sexual abuse, or open drunkenness, or hunger or cold, or denial of love – which they hadn't – to acquire dull habits of secrecy and shame. Children hear their parents fighting and think it's their fault, and go and hide within themselves. What could be more banal?

In rural Ireland, back then, Sundays were still Sundays. Sunday mornings were the worst. There would be the folk

Mass in the parish church at noon, the family at home all day, and school again tomorrow. The tensions and set pieces . . . There is a reason why Irish writers keep serving up fights at family dinners. The pieties . . . For the rest of his life, he would hate the sound of the theme music from *Sunday Miscellany*, a weekly arts show, on the kitchen radio, of its poems and prose pieces, read in liturgical tones, and the passages of worthy, woollen music that were played between the readings. As a boy, he had believed, with complete certainty, that even if he were stranded alone for years on a desert island, with no calendar to mark the days, he would still know when Sunday came around again, just from the feel of it, the beige hopelessness in the air. It would feel like the theme tune from *Sunday Miscellany*.

As children, they all turned furtive; the secret war between their parents, and their parents' efforts to protect them from seeing it, seeped into them like second-hand smoke. He himself had acquired a parallel addiction, to stealing biscuits. It helped to pass the time to always have a treat in store. Whenever biscuits were brought into the house, he would ferret out their hiding place, stake them out for a while, then enter the packet through the back, so a casual glance would not register the theft. Eventually, when the biscuits were all or mostly gone, a parent would reach for what they thought was a full packet. Then there'd be raised voices and slaps and punishments, and guilt. Years later, after alcohol, women, adventure and drugs had replaced biscuits on his shopping list, he understood that the guilt had always been part of his game.

He and his wife operated by different rules, now. There was no real anger with their girls when stashes of confectionary were found to have been compromised. Mostly just humorous reproaches and the clicking of tongues, and sometimes a cut in the next official ration of the chocolate they shared in front of the TV, if the parents still chose to remember the crime. It was up to them, the adults, to hide the stuff better; if the children could find it, weren't they kind of entitled to take a cut? It was the same with his razors, lately; as the only male in a house with three females, it was his responsibility to squirrel away his means of shaving; what else could you expect a gang of women to do, if they found his good razor, but use it to saw away at things much coarser than his face, blunting it and clogging it and warping the blades? He flattered himself that, thanks to his thing with the biscuits, he knew a lot about hiding stuff, that he was poacher turned gamekeeper. When, inevitably, he was proven wrong again, he would make a formal protest, but accept the defeat more or less philosophically. My face is bleeding. Touché. Because why should children have to feel guilty about trivial things, the way he'd felt guilty all through his life because he'd hated family Sundays, and Mass, and folksy literature, and school, and had eaten all those delicious biscuits? He took himself way too seriously. How could he not laugh at this now, when he had children of his own and could see that, however badly they behaved, however cruel and selfish they could be in their innocence, however vexatious and crafty, and careless with his razors, to him they would always be blameless and lovely, and that he must have been lovely and blameless once too.

The second road trip he made after his Dublin paper first sent him to Africa, the one after Goma, was to Somalia. There was a local interest: the Irish army had sent a transport unit to run convoys for an Indian brigade serving with the United Nations. The Indians were securing the lawless central region around Baidoa, Somalia's second city, and protecting the humanitarian organisations that had come to relieve the Somali famine, but instead found themselves targets for looting, abduction and ambush in a bewildering clan-based civil war.

How he'd loved himself on that trip to Baidoa. He was fascinated by the idea of deserts, having grown up amid dripping hedgerows, but he had never been in one before; Somalia was pretty much a desert. The American military had stirred up a wasps' nest and then pulled out, but the UN still held strong points around Mogadishu, hunkered down excitingly, like outposts in the world of Mad Max. Gunmen sniped at each other across the landing zone in the main UN compound, but they were so far away that it was considered polite to ignore them. Was he *under fire*? He sort of was!

He was flown to Baidoa by an ex-British-army helicopter pilot, who, hearing his Irish accent, let him sit beside him in the cockpit so they could talk over the intercom. They flew at top speed, ten feet above the Mogadishu–Baidoa highway, as the pilot reminisced about his old days in Northern Ireland. He said he liked the IRA because they'd made his life more interesting. Through the glass bubbles in the chin of the helicopter, they saw wild pigs and feral camels bolting into the acacias. Rounding a bend, they came upon a gang of Somali gunmen on the back of a technical – a flatbed truck mounting an anti-aircraft cannon. The gunmen had to duck for their lives as the helicopter swept just over their heads. The pilot was laughing and whooping as they flew on their way. And he told himself, he actually said this internally, and not for the last time: It's never too late to have a happy childhood. You could definitely say that things went to his head.

The term 'embed' hadn't yet been invented, but he was embedded with the Irish transport unit. This must have been a pain in the arse for its small team of officers, so they palmed him off for a day on the Indian Army, to which they were subordinate in the UN chain of command. The Indian Army, famous for their slow, old-fashioned, elaborate hospitality,

would soak up some of his time with briefings and demon-
strations. And so, on the morning of 31 August 1994, he was
driven to Baidoa's new hospital, set up and run by the Indian
medical corps. There wasn't much chance of a story in this,
but he made some notes anyway, mostly for stage business,
as he was shown around the wards, talking to military nurses
and doctors, and to their Somali assistants, who interpreted
for him with shy local patients. He thought he was done
with the hospital, then, but it turned out there would be one
more formality. Protocol demanded that, before he left, the
esteemed reporter should sit with the unit's commander.
So he was shown into an air-conditioned tent in the yard of
the hospital, between the main building and the high wall
separating it from the street, where the medical colonel had
set up his office. The colonel sat him down and offered him
fruit juice, and modestly described the excellent work of his
women and men. As he talked, two diffident young majors
arrived in the back of the tent. The colonel introduced his
two senior surgeons, who had come for a scheduled manage-
ment meeting. They too made some small talk. Four hours
later, when it suddenly became important, he couldn't recall
anything of what had been said. He'd been too impatient to
be on his way.

Once honour was satisfied, the doctors could get back
to their life-saving business. His Indian driver took him to

the brigade HQ to meet the brigadier, whose adjutant gave a tactical briefing, with lots of wax pencil symbols on map overlays. He was next shown around the cells of the local hellhole prison, which the Indians were taking in charge, and where, bewilderingly, the pornographic drawings on the walls featured camels, not women. Then they took him to see the orphanage and school they had set up for displaced Somali children. What happens to these kids when your mission ends? he'd asked the young Muslim captain in charge of the orphanage, just for something to say. He watched the young captain trying not to cry.

The last item on the agenda was a helicopter tour of the brigade's area of operations. He'd been looking forward to that all day. So they went to the helicopter terminal, at the airport, and watched an Indian military Alouette being fuelled for his jaunt. They were still waiting, a few minutes later, when the crew sprinted out to the helicopter, took off without him, and began circling and swooping over some distant point in downtown Baidoa. And just as he was beginning to accept, with a petulant feeling, that for some bullshit reason there would be no chopper ride for him today, word came through that the UN's civilian helicopters were also to be scrambled, for medevac flights to Mogadishu. There had been an attack at the hospital in town.

Jeeps and trucks arrived at the airport in convoy and

unloaded three stretchers, with three zippered body bags. These were surrounded, on the apron, by Indian staff from the hospital, by captains and lieutenants, women and men, nurses and doctors, who stood around the bodies, embracing and weeping. Then they cancelled the medevac flights, the helicopters that would have rushed the three victims, had they still been alive, to Mogadishu for surgery. No such procedures were available in Baidoa, for the time being, because the colonel in command of the hospital, and both of his surgeons, had just been killed by a rifle grenade, fired into their tent by persons unknown, as they were holding a meeting.

He would have thought, before it happened, that he would have been more moved, enlarged, enlightened, by his first near encounter with violent death, by having been in the wrong place with the wrong people, though not quite at the wrong time. That's how it works in the books and the movies: you learn from stuff like that. He'd also have thought that he would remember their faces, but he didn't, even a short time later, as hard as he tried. He hadn't taken proper notes of their meeting, which had been, in his view, just a courtesy call. And one day, much later, when he was looking back over his life for sliding-door moments, and when he realised that it was twenty-six years to the day since this episode in Somalia, the Internet didn't know their names either. The only reference he could see to the incident online was a pdf of his own short news report, hidden behind the *Irish Times* paywall, and even that was hard to find. The hospital commander was named in his piece as Lieutenant Colonel Chittaranjan Panda, no age, no marital status. The surgeons were simply Major Dutta and Major Lal. This looked like weak reporting on his part, as if he'd taken their surnames from a press release issued by the Indian Army, which, being brisk and formal in such matters, hadn't bothered with their first names. His reporting had been poor, there was no getting around that. But he'd been new at that kind of work, and back then you couldn't fill in any gaps in your on-the-spot news-gathering by sending off emails, or looking up details online. He'd always worked for daily papers; as deadlines approached, you just went with what you had.

That was then, this was now. He did another online search, this time with a range of keywords taken from his own article – Dutta, Lal, Panda, 320 Field Ambulance Unit. Nothing. If only they'd died a year or two later, when everything suddenly became known forever. Yet it struck him now, looking back at the past through his new online lens, that the biggest omission from his report wasn't the full names and personal details of the dead men – their families, their humanising details – though these were badly lacking. The missing element was himself; it was the fact that he had left out any direct mention of his own involvement in that day. No *I was there*. No attempt to presume on the dead men's acquaintance, to claim a piece of their deaths, to make it sound as if he'd made a human connection with them, however briefly, before they were transformed into tragic heroes. Imagine that now, in the age of social media, when everything is *Look at me*. Even back then, in those more impersonal times, he would have been entitled to plant his *I* in the heart of the story, given how close he'd been to it that day. But, now he thought about it, twenty-six years later, it wasn't a story that he'd told many people, then or since. In fact, he couldn't remember telling it to anyone at all. Yet it was a good story, and it was true. And now he thought about it some more, there had been other close calls, closer than that one, that he hadn't talked about much either. Incidents that he had difficulty remembering himself, as if his inner search tab was broken and he had to perform a manual search, item by item, on each of those rare occasions when he needed to dig them out. The only one he'd ever talked about, in the bar, or wherever, was that amateur ambush in the coup in Lesotho, that time one of his colleagues was actually shot – Kiley, as it happened – though he'd not been badly hurt. Which made it Kiley's story, not his.

Was he playing it cool? Was he too modest, or too unflappable, to boast about his own real-life adventures? He might have told himself that before. But now, in the light of the year he'd been having, he understood that what he really felt was a kind of embarrassment. You could even say shame. He felt guilty that his own experiences hadn't felt to him like they should, like they do in the books and the movies. He'd stopped watching television news, not long after Goma, because he'd discovered that the terrible things he'd seen for himself looked even worse later, when he saw them again on the screen. They looked too real. While trying to test himself against what he thought was reality, he had, ironically, been discounting anything that happened to him personally, anything that he'd seen or done, as not being serious, not really worth remembering. Bigger things happened to other people, or on the page or the screen. Anything that he'd done was no longer important. Any club that he joined was no longer worth belonging to. And he understood, now, that it had been the same with his relationships. Every new one had been damaged from the start, because how could you be honest with someone whom you felt, deep down, you must have tricked into liking you? Maybe that's another reason why he'd been so inexplicably upset when Charlotte was suddenly no longer out there, off in the distance. She hadn't given him time to do anything to hurt her. Maybe she'd played him onside.

If so, her death had finally pricked this bubble. More than one bubble, maybe. He saw, now, that no adventure he'd had, no achievement, no drug, no affair, no gamble he'd made, winning or losing, nothing he had written or could ever hope to write, could compare with the simple fact of her having faced death, with full foreknowledge, quietly, bravely and young, leaving her children behind her. Perhaps he should cut himself some slack: perhaps he could excuse himself a little for all that self-indulgence, for having romanticised her, post mortem, decades after she'd stopped being real to him. What could be more heroic than the way she had died?

You step out into the street, looking at your phone, and you hear a horn blaring, and you jump back again, quickly, just before the bus hits you, and your heart races for three minutes, and then you're back to being you. There is only one sliding door, and the only question is how and when we go through it. Such were his best stories. Everybody has them. He'd been wise to keep them to himself.

He'd first met his wife in Dublin, before he went to Africa, when he was dating her best friend. They hadn't got on. She seemed to think he was arrogant, which annoyed her. He thought she was aggressive. A few years later he met her again, when he was home on leave from Africa. He was walking along Burgh Quay when she stepped out of a bus queue and said hello. He was surprised how friendly she was. He had thought she didn't like him. She was now working for his old paper, and a year or so later it sent her to Durban to cover a conference. They saw a lot of each other in and around the conference centre, and did some light sparring, like they had the first time they'd met. He was in the process of winding things up and moving back to Ireland; he had become tired and scared of his life as it was then, and thought, on the basis of absolutely no research at all, that he could make a new living writing literary fiction. He still had enough arrogance in him for that.

Not long after he returned to Ireland, he called her on her mobile. They went for dinner in the Trocadero, and to a gig in the Olympia. The Cowboy Junkies. Afterwards, she became very quiet, and, unable to read her feelings, he had to ask her, formally, if he had her permission to flirt with her. She said that he had. So that's how it started. A little on edge.

Soon after they began dating, they almost split up. He'd stayed the night at her house in Stoneybatter, and, as she was getting ready to leave for work in the morning, they had a row. It was about nothing important, nothing he could remember (and what did it say about him that he got in these rows, but could never remember them?), but she did have a quick temper, even quicker than his; she had her own dark place, which he liked. He told her he was leaving, and she told him he could go for good, as far as she was concerned. He was surprised at how brutally she said it, her black finality.

He hadn't seen this coming. They'd been getting on so well. There'd been quite a lot of hormones.

But he'd been in this place before. Walking down Stoney-batter, on his way home to Broadstone, he had second thoughts. It was Valentine's Day, as it happened. He went into the Centra on the corner of Brunswick Street, the one that was then run by a crowd of South Africans, with their familiar accents, and he bought a Valentine's card and a biro, and – because he knew that it would have to fit through a letter box – one of those thin little bars of Terry's Chocolate Orange. He wrote *Happy Valentine's Day* in the card, signed a question mark underneath it, and then a single X, put the chocolate bar into the envelope, walked back to Mount Temple Road and posted it through her door. When he called her that evening she was ready to forgive him. It didn't matter for what. Sometimes, he still believed back then, you just stick a plaster on things and move on.

He'd started work on what would turn out, eight years later, to be his first novel, and he was trying to make ends meet by freelance reporting for overseas papers. But he'd miscalculated. He was never going to make a living that way in Ireland; there wasn't enough news of international interest. But his Australian papers, which hadn't replaced him after he decided to leave Johannesburg, asked him to go back to Africa a couple of times that year, to cover the crisis in Zimbabwe. He was banned from that country, but knew how to sneak in. This brought in a little money, but his savings were running out, and he still had a mortgage. He would have to get a proper job, a prospect that dismayed him; he hadn't worked in an office for many years. Then, one day, he got a phone call from Australia. Would he consider going to Jerusalem, to be their Middle East correspondent, for a good full-time salary and all expenses paid?

Africa and the Middle East were similar beats, in terms of the skills they required. Some of his friends from Johannesburg had already moved on to Jerusalem. Also, there was going to be a big war in Iraq, the kind that most reporters would give anything to cover. But hadn't he had enough of that already? And there was another complication.

He sat down with her, the next day, and told her he'd been offered a job that seemed too good to refuse. But he also told her, for the first time, that he loved her, and hoped they could stay together. If she thought they couldn't manage for a while, being apart most of the time, he'd turn down the offer. It was the first time he saw her cry. A few months later, she came out to join him, and to freelance on her own account. Their two children were conceived in their flat on the Green Line. The job paid off the mortgage on the house they moved back to, six years later, when he'd had enough again. Back in Ireland, he stayed at home and wrote a bit, and learned to cook adequate meals, and took care of the babies. She went back to work and became the main earner. Apart from all the late-night feeds and sleeplessness and bickering, this turned into a quiet, loving and mostly happy life. And he had to add a new self-reproach to his catalogue, for having to remind himself, still, from time to time, in spite of the fact that it was so glaringly obvious, how very lucky he'd been. He thought of all the health scares that none of them had ever had, yet. Some close escapes were worth bearing in mind.

There was a phrase that he never put into a search engine, that spring and summer, though he was often tempted. Midlife crisis. He understood that he was a cliché, but he still wanted to go along for the ride, with no map and no cheat codes, no spoilers. He'd learned what every teenage self-harmer knows: that sometimes it's better to feel something than nothing. Plus, he still wasn't quite ready to let go of the delusion that he was special, to admit that there was nothing rare or tragic about his experience. He would do this, like most people, quietly and alone, the way he'd always done these things before.

One day, online, he saw a young female writer joke about how middle-aged men are ridiculous, because they always think they're the first one to go through this sort of experience. He wanted to answer, Well, it *is* the first time for each one of them. Also, he wasn't sure that these things were gendered, the way this writer seemed to think. Women are also not fond of ageing, and grief, and illness and loss. But in the end he didn't send his reply. She'd find out in her own time. And if you thought about it, what was wrong with laughing at the old fools? At a certain stage in life – and you don't know what might trigger it, what beat of a wing, a blue butterfly on a hospital door – you have to accept that your past is gone and you're running low on future, that there will be no escape for you from time. You're trapped. You're the sap in your own sitcom. What sane response can there be but to laugh?

They went swimming in the sea a lot that August, on holiday in Kerry, and then on Inishbofin. But, back in Dublin, the girls were now too big for the shallow beach at Dollymount, where the tide could retreat halfway out to the horizon. So they started going to Donabate instead. It was easy to reach from their side of the city, and you could swim there at any state of the tide. They would park by the hotel and walk on to the long, gently curving strand. Lambay Island to the east of them. Howth Head to the south. He'd started following his daughters into the sea, though he dreaded the last stretch of the journey, the naked walk in the wind to the edge of the water, the sting in his toes, the first cold slap of the waves above his knees, then up over his crotch to his belly and chest. But he knew that all these troubles would vanish as soon as he counted to three and dived under the water. He came up with a mantra that he repeated, inwardly, to steel himself for this moment, as he picked his way barefoot across the sand and crushed seashells: I will be reborn. It had a pleasing, self-mocking pomposity, a cod-baptismal sound. But it was also true: from one moment to the next you could become a new person, clear in your mind, past the stage of shivering, and ready to swim. You might as well get it over with. You're already up to your chest in the sea.

September

September Girls

That's how a writer might end it. A wistful parable. A hint of redemption. A story of life going on, counterpointing the turn of the season from summer to fall. Faraway beaches, echoing in time. Boys of Summer. September Gurls. That's how a writer might try to sneak away from their own story, but in real life there is no such easy way out.

A writer would try to trick you, and in the process, trick themselves. They might swear to themselves to tell you nothing but the truth, as far as they can fix it, but their memory might let them down. They might feel it necessary to leave some things out and to change a few details, to protect people's feelings – and most of all, their own. They might even have started out just wanting to write something nice for some people they knew once, a few words to keep them around for a little while longer, and then felt obliged to go into a lot of other stuff they'd have otherwise let lie, just to give themselves some cover for talking out of turn.

And a writer might also hold some things back, either for narrative effect or because they couldn't stand to face them until they had no choice. On the night that Charlotte died, he had gone downstairs to tell his wife the news, but she had already heard from someone else. He told her, numbly, that he hadn't even known that Charlotte was ill again, much less that she was dying. But his wife looked at him strangely, and she said, Yes, you did. And he said, No, I didn't. And she said, Yes, you did. Seán told you she was probably dying, in the pub, on Christmas Eve. And he said, No, he didn't. I never heard that. But he was already beginning to wonder if maybe he had heard it, and had somehow blanked out the crucial information, as he had so many times before. Except this would be so much more monstrous, if it was done before the fact, not after it. So he tried to remember if he'd heard that she was dying and had suppressed the information, or filed it and forgotten it. Had he heard, and not really cared at the time? He really didn't think that was possible. But, though he tortured his memory, he didn't know for sure. He only knew that he felt guilty – but then again, he usually did.

It was already apparent, only minutes after he'd heard the bad news, that his failure to say a simple hello/goodbye would prove costly, especially at night, for some time to come. Had he had his chance, and blown it? He knew that Charlotte herself would scarcely have cared, one way or the other. Knowing that didn't help, though. Had he done this to himself?

His wife, seeing how stricken he looked, quickly backtracked, out of kindness. Maybe he hadn't heard, she said. Maybe Seán had told her, but he hadn't been listening to that part of the conversation. The pub was loud. He had terrible hearing. He might have been zoned out on the edge of their group, the way he so often was. It didn't matter, she said. But it did.

He'd meant to end the thing in August, to leave it on that beach. Then one night in September his phone pinged. Sarah had sent him a scan of a photograph she'd found in a forgotten stash. It showed Charlotte and Tommy and himself, all sitting together on a low futon couch. Charlotte, in the middle, looks achingly lovely and poised, with a glass of red wine and her sardonic smile. She is wearing hoop earrings and her green Lycra dress. Tommy sits forward, animated and handsome, gesturing with a cigarette. He himself is slumped at the end of the futon, beside and behind Charlotte, arms folded defensively, his knees looming in the foreground, so that you can only see the top of his head. Just think, wrote Sarah in the accompanying message, two of those three young people are dead.

Sarah said she also had the reverse angle photograph, taken by Tommy a few moments before or after, showing herself and some more of their people on the opposite side of the room. It was Charlotte's future husband who took the photograph that Sarah sent him.

So now he had, after all, a photograph of himself with Charlotte, from their short time together, a long time ago. It hurt now to think of them all, happy there together, but here was the evidence, a last-minute twist. But what did it prove? We were. That's all. It was good. And some of us continue. Could any true story end any other way?

Acknowledgements

This book was written with the help of generous bursaries from the Arts Council of Ireland and the Canada Council for the Arts.

Thanks to Nuala Haughey, Gabrielle Hetherington, Róisín O'Loughlin and both John O'Loughlins for having the kindness and strength to read early drafts and comment on them. Special thanks to Nuala and my daughters for their company and love in a strange time.

Jeroen Kramer shared his thoughts and insights, and gave me permission to quote at length from his wonderful book, *Room 103*, in the third chapter, 'The Rain Queen'.

This book quotes lines from the following songs: Chapter one, Undecided: 'Do Your Own Time', by A.C. Newman,

'Ceremony', by Joy Division/New Order, and 'Tomorrow', by Ladytron; Chapter four, someone who writes: 'Bonny' and 'Couldn't Bear to be Special' by Paddy McAloon of Prefab Sprout; Chapter seven, In Another Life: 'Once in a Lifetime', by Talking Heads.

Thanks to my agent, Peter Straus, and to my publishers: Jon Riley, Jasmine Palmer and all at riverrun in London; Michelle MacAleese, Bruce Walsh, Douglas Richmond, Sarah MacLachlan and the people of House of Anansi Books in Toronto. Penny Price did an excellent copy edit, and Jack Smyth conceived and designed a beautiful cover.

A version of Chapter five, 'Stars of Bethlehem', first appeared in issue 11 of Banshee Journal. Thanks to Laura Cassidy, Claire Hennessy and Eimear Ryan.

Thanks also to Conn Ó Midheach, Allsún nic Gearailt, Kevin Power, Nicola Byrne, Peadar O'Mahony and Kevin McCarthy.

This work is based on my own impressions and memories, such as they are. Others may well remember things differently.